VALIANT
BOOK OF EXTREMELY ANCIENT ALIENS

MW01284368

VALIANT THOR'S
BOOK OF EXTREMELY ANCIENT ALIENS

EDITED BY

GRAY BARKER

ANDREW B. COLVIN

NEW SAUCERIAN BOOKS, POINT PLEASANT, WEST VIRGINIA

Other Books by Valiant Thor

The Art of Ascension: Achieving Communion With God and Creation

Fantastic Beings and Where to Find Them: How to Contact Space Aliens, Intelligences, and People

In Days to Come: The Escape of the Stranger at the Pentagon (with Gray Barker)

Millennium Seven: Biblical Secrets for Galactic Ascension in the 21st Century

Our Spacecraft Over Your Earth: The Stranger From the Pentagon Speaks

Outwitting Tomorrow: Secrets For Living From the Great Pyramid (with Dr. Frank E. Stranges)

Sips of Truth: Decoding the Dead Sea Scrolls and Other Biblical Mysteries

Starseeds of Hollywood: My Venusian Ascension With Valiant Thor (with Lee Crandall)

Strangers From the the Pentagon: The UFO Conspiracy (with Dr. Frank E. Stranges)

Valiant Thor's Book of Relationships: Love, Health, and Success Through Interplanetary Awareness

Valiant Thor's Venusian Health Magic: The Vitality of Vril

Valiant Thor's Venusian Science Secrets: The Supreme Technology of the Ascended Masters

Valiant Thor's Book of Extremely Ancient Aliens

ISBN-13: 978-1548778705
ISBN-10: 1548778702

©2017 New Saucerian, LLC

PUBLISHED BY: New Saucerian Books – Point Pleasant, West Virginia

CONTENTS

INTRODUCTION

During the last few hundred years, humanity's ideas about the environment, both local and universal, have undergone a complete change. The discovery of the Americas, the growth of trade through the world, and the development of communications on land, sea, and in the air have enabled people thousands of miles apart to get together very quickly. Our people oversaw these human advancements, from our orbiting platforms, and approved of them.

With international cables and telefaxes, important business can be resolved without long journeys or physical meetings. Radio and television have made it possible for millions of people to hear and see what is happening on the other side of the planet. It can certainly be stated that modern technology has very nearly made nonsense of distance.

Now you are on the verge of your greatest achievement and most magnificent adventure – exploring our solar system and universe, an area so vast that your planet is like a grain of sand in the Sahara Desert. Your ideas of outer space have expanded. Leading astronomers such as Sir Fred Hoyle, Carl Sagan, and Jacques Vallee have expressed their opinion that millions of planets in the Milky Way may be inhabited by intelligent sentient beings.

Some flying saucers students are coming around to the viewpoint that humanity was seeded on this planet from elsewhere. There are references in the Bible and other ancient writings to "gods" coming to Earth and mating with the daughters of men. This should be an obvious clue to our cultural interrelationships. Perhaps when we finally make the great journey into space, together, contact will be made with other races of the universe. What a tremendous moment that will be.

I myself have postulated that there are universes beside our own in the vast cosmos. Further, these other universes, or dimensions, interpenetrate our own, and are most likely occupied by creatures and beings that can become visible to us under special conditions. How we see them, and how they see us, may depend on one's own particular frame of reference. There is nothing necessarily "spooky" ghostly about this concept, as the beings involved may *not* be apparitions or disembodied souls. They may be intelligent lifeforms, just like us.

Perhaps it is true that the Great Architect created man in his own image – what are called the "Sons of God" in the Bible. These beings were perfect, and operated in four distinct areas of the divine mind: the creative, the etheric, the astral, and the analytic. It is quite possible that these Sons of God created a microcosm using their God-given powers, which was a reflection of the macrocosm. It is within this microcosm that we dwell.

The sacred book of the Maya, *The Popol Vuh*, as well as the Egyptian Book of the Dead and several Tibetan, Babylonian, and Sumerian sources, tell of "gods" that made this universe. These were all monotheistic cultures, yet they recognized that "gods" made the universe!

When you finally make contact with other races from inside or outside our solar system, we will find that they, too, were put there by the "gods." While we may all vary in certain degrees, with some ETs being more advanced (or even less evolved), it is likely that we are all derived from the same universal source.

It is now believed that for every atomic particle, like the neutron, electron, and proton, there exists another particle of the same mass, but with an equal and opposite electric charge. Such anti-particles are called antimatter, and when they meet their opposite number, the two simply disappear in a puff of energy, leaving no trace. This is what scientists have discovered in their experiments in so-called "cloud chambers" or "particle accelerators."

Astronomers have come up with clues to support the experiments of the physicists. Radio astronomers have discovered far-out evidence of a collision between two galaxies – a gigantic highway accident on the cosmic interstate. Antimatter gives rise to some interesting conjecture. There may exist a kind of looking-glass universe in which all matter, as we know it, is made up of antimatter. A thin curtain is all that separates us, and it occasionally makes itself visible to each side.

Recently, attention has become focused on what are called quasars, or quasi-stellar objects. Far beyond the Milky Way, there are huge lumps of matter releasing enormous quantities of ultraviolet light. Each lump is about equal to a million of our suns put together. The energy each gives off is considered to be 100 times greater than that from any other known object in the sky.

Emilio Segre, the Nobel Prize winner, expressed the view that there must be a parallel development between the worlds of matter and antimatter. He once stated: "The principle of symmetry postulates the evidence of particles and anti-particles in equal numbers, which signifies equal quantities of matter and antimatter in the universe. Some of the galaxies we see may be anti-galaxies, consisting of anti-stars circled by anti-planets.

For years, physicists have sought some contradiction to matter. If matter has a positive charge, then something with a negative charge ought to exist somewhere to cancel it out. This brings up the exciting thought that such a universe of antimatter may exist and be interpenetrating our own. Have the courage to peek through the curtain, and you will find countless wonders.

-Valiant Thor, 1983

FOREWORD

If the microcosm is a reflection of the macrocosm, it should have polarity. It seems therefore reasonable that our universe should have a neighbor of opposite polarity in the microcosm. The distinguished German scientist, F.L. Boschke, in his book *Creation Still Goes On*, asks why should matter and antimatter not have been created simultaneously?

He refers to the work of C.J. Keveane, a physicist at the University of Arizona, who published one of the first theories of creation that included antimatter. According to Keveane, matter and antimatter were united at the moment of creation, and their separation followed later, because between them were the mutually repellant forces of gravity and antigravity.

Sooner or later, our scientists will produce a new theory of the universe that will include both matter and antimatter. Is it possible that some of the flying saucers come from the parallel universe of antimatter? Have the inhabitants of our neighboring universe found the means to get here without disintegrating themselves or us?

It is notable that some reported contacts with UFO occupants are "workmanlike" and leave no offensive odors or symptoms. Others however, seem clumsy and leave unpleasant smells and physical maladies. Could it be that our next-door neighbors are not quite up to the techniques of the "gods?" Or are they just as clueless about what is happening as we are?

Our knowledge is growing by leaps and bounds, but it is still very elementary. Every fresh discovery poses a thousand new questions. One thing is certain: humanity will never be satisfied until all the answers have been found. And since it is unlikely that the answers will ever be found, men will struggle with dissatisfaction. What we have achieved is but the beginning of an extremely long and occasionally painful journey that may – if we are lucky – take us to realms beyond our wildest dreams.

The following reports by Saucerian Press correspondents and editors demonstrate the wide range of thought concerning "ancient astronauts" or "aliens." We recommend that you pick up their books, many of which are currently being republished by our new book unit at Saucerian ("New Saucerian" – a unification of our earlier "New Age" and "Saucerian" presses). The thought that mankind was seeded from the stars is an enduring belief, replete with alternative views and approaches. In this volume, we asked the illustrious Venusian thinker, Valiant Thor, to choose his favorite Saucerian articles.

I am reminded of the case of Antonio Villas Boas, the Brazilian farmer who, twenty years ago, famously made contact with the people of the "Bird Planet," who forced him to mate with a beautiful blonde aboard a flying saucer. How is this different than the tales from the Bible, where the "daughters of men" mated with the giant birdmen, or Anunnaki or Nephilim, from outer space? And what about Mothman reportedly appearing in the bedrooms of young females in West Virginia, keeping in instant telepathic contact with them and their young "genius" children?

What does it all mean? As Erich von Daniken likes to say, there are many paths to climb when it comes to Ancient Aliens. We tend to like the more extreme theories, naturally. Perhaps we have been in this business too long, and it takes a little more to shock us. But when you think about it, the simple possibility that ancient astronauts are carefully watching and manipulating us is quite a terrifying prospect, in and of itself.

-Gray Barker, 1983

CHAPTER 1

THE PERILS OF ERASING ASTROLOGY FROM THE PAST – INGO
SWANN – 1980

Astrology is perhaps the most detested topic of the modern scientific age.
Nevertheless, it is generally agreed that various kinds of astrology played
significant social roles in most past civilizations and their cultures. There
is no historical argument at all regarding the fact that the roots of modern
astrology are found in very ancient Egypt, India, China, and Arabia, and
among the ancient Mediterranean civilizations of Babylon, Macedonia,
Greece, Italy, Palestine, and so forth.

It is also generally agreed that few ancient rulers took many steps without
consulting astrologers, although they are considered silly by moderns for
having done so. It is also known that in most of those very ancient and less
ancient societies, astrology was considered a state function largely held in
the hands of state-supported priesthoods.

The social, political, and religious influence of astrology can be traced
forward in time, through the Middle Ages and the Renaissance, and into
early modern times. For example, in *Prophecy and Power: Astrology in
Early Modern England,* the scholar Patrick Curry traces the fortunes and
misfortunes of astrology in early modern England from about 1642 to
about 1835. This well-researched text clearly establishes that astrology
was at least an often-vital influence among the nobility and intellectuals
responsible for shaping cultural and governmental policies.

This "vital influence" dates backward in time, into prehistory. In the case of
Egypt, for example, elements of astrological practice are evident in the early
dynastic period, approximately 3000 B.C. In this sense, then, astrology has
at least a 5000-year known history of strategic influence, which endured,
in various forms and intensity, until about 1830 A.D. Of all social and
cultural phenomena, then, astrology has been consistently, and sometimes
prominently, present throughout human history.

The historical presence of astrology is seldom argued. What is argued,
though, is whether historical and archaeological attention should be paid
to it. Both history and archaeology, as we take them in their modern sense,
are scientific processes. As such, the two disciplines, both having the goal of
revealing the past, however near or distant, are subject not only to scientific
methodologies, but also to scientific overviews, and the "realities," concepts,
and preconceptions upon which those overviews are constructed.

It is abundantly clear that modern science rejected astrology, and, in fact, many scientists evinced pride in so doing. The ostensible cultural reasons for the rejection comprise a complex tale, but the general scientific justification held that the planets were too far away from Earth to have any virtual effect upon its geological, biological, or human psychological phenomena.

In this sense, then, astrology was not scientific, and not deemed either a credible or an appropriate topic for scientific study or analysis. It was stigmatized as such not only scientifically, but socially as well.

Thus, when historians and archaeologists attached their disciplines to science proper, the astrological stigmatization had to be observed, or at least danced around, in order to maintain scientific credibility and acceptance. The result is that the term "astrology" does not at all figure in scientific, historical, or archaeological frames of reference, and if so, then only in a pejorative sense.

The fallout from this modern anti-astrological situation is that, in large measure, no scientist, historian, or archaeologist has studied astrology, its mechanics, or its various stages of past historical and archaeological development. In fact, the presence in history and in past cultures of astrology is bowdlerized from modern historical and archaeological perspectives and applied anachronistically into the past.

Since many past cultures indeed contained significant astrological socializing cores, it is questionable whether contemporary historians or archaeologists working to reconstruct the past as accurately as possible can really do so by excising astrology from it. "Bleeping" astrology out of history and archaeology serves no valid purpose in either discipline, whose mutual interacting goals are to study the past as completely as possible.

Modern historians and archaeologists who know nothing of astrology are not capable of even recognizing astrological elements in the past cultures they select for study. Such historians and archaeologists need not themselves believe in astrology; but many of the past societies they select for study did carry various astrological beliefs within them, and how these latter are to be correctly interpreted or identified by the former (if the former possess no astrological database) is a matter of some (often humorous) interest.

One significant and telling clue exists regarding the utter importance of astrology to the past. Furthermore, it is one upon which all scientists, historians, archaeologists, and astrologers agree. Prior to the middle modern age (beginning circa 1845), nothing in previous human history indicates that any division existed between astronomy and what we call astrology. It is fair to say, though, that the astrological portion of astronomy had its philosophical detractors in antiquity. But a clinical inspection of the "complaints" of these detractors shows that they inveighed more against the fraudulent-divinatory use of astronomy than astronomical astrology per se.

The beginning of the formal cultural-scientific separation of astrology from astronomy is difficult to date, but it probably began during the Renaissance, when Count Pico de Mirandola (1463-94) argued pervasively against the former and an anti-astrological cult formed as a result. The completed separation occurred sometime after the death of Sir Isaac Newton (1642-1727), one of the greatest scientist-astronomers of his age, and an "astrologer." As the scholar Patrick Curry shows, astrology-cum-astronomy remained a vital intellectual force in early modern England until after about 1830.

The term astrology itself is of rather recent vintage when compared to the whole of "astrological" history. A number of linguistic contributions are involved, which makes the origin of the term difficult to identify. There is no easy way to sort out the difficulties, but the complexities are eased somewhat if we bear in mind that what we call "astronomy" and "astrology" were considered one and the same thing up until at least the late Renaissance, when a few individuals began to define between the study of the planets and stars per se (astronomy) and the study of their effects on Earth (astrology).

Linguistic evidence shows that, although the Romans considered astronomy and astrology as synonymous, they did discriminate between *astronomia*, which took on a scientific sense, and *astrologia*, which took on a "star-divinatory" sense. But this division in no way carried the same cultural impact as our present use of the two terms does.

The acquisition into English of "astronomy" derives from the Old European astronomia, an obvious carry-over from the Latin. Astrologia was subsequently reintroduced (it is thought) as referring to the practical application of astronomia to mundane affairs, and thus gradually limited during the eighteenth century to reputed influences of the stars unknown to science.

It is worth noting that Shakespeare (1546-1616), the arch-innovator of the English language and neologisms, did not utilize the term "astrology," and so it can definitely be stated that it was not in popular, intellectual, or fringe use until sometime after his death.

The modern definitions of astrology and astronomy have separated the two in dramatic ways. The retrospective application of the differences into antiquity is clearly an anachronistic exercise that mollifies contemporary anti-astrological sentiments – but which distorts our view of social configurations of past cultures. Many aspects of the past (oral traditions, written records, artifacts, and monuments) cannot be completely understood by sanitizing them of their astrological connotations.

In his remarkable book, *The Case For Astrology*, the astrological archaeologist John Anthony West, discussed two matters extremely important for historians and archaeologists. He shows that all of the scientific objections to astrology have been refuted or answered not by astrologers, but by the analogous work of other scientists. These refutations and answers, it should be noted, go unacknowledged behind the anti-astrological sentiments that still prevail.

In any case, West clearly establishes the two fundamental premises of "astrology," and shows that these can be found complete in pre-dynastic Egypt, and that this extremely early completeness suggests an even earlier origin of the two premises. All of astrology – pre-historical, historical, or contemporary – is based upon a simple two-part premise: 1) that correlations exist between celestial and terrestrial events; and 2) that correspondences exist between the position of the planets at birth and the human personality. To these two premises another must be added, 3) that the correlations and correspondences manifest on a spectrum ranging from beneficent to malevolent, constructive to destructive, angelic to demonic, or, as often expressed in contemporary astrology, from negative to positive.

Now, it must be stated that belief in either the reality or correctness of these premises is not necessary to understanding how earlier cultures regarded them, or why they regarded them at all. As a famous Mayan archaeologist recently noted, the Mayans did not design their societies for our approval or even with our understanding in mind, but rather within the scope of their own realities, whether these are silly, disgusting, laudatory, or alien to us.

The first premise given above approximates what may have been meant, in antiquity, by astronomy or celestial watching (although no definition of astronomy has come down to us). The repeating cycles of celestial activity have correlations with terrestrial events, and so the earliest vestiges of celestial-watching most obviously had to do with practical matters – especially those of a forecasting type.

There is no functional definitional difference between "forecasting" and "divining," except possibly the methods used to arrive at either. Indeed, the calendar is not just a day-keeping mechanism, but a forecasting or divining tool that shows us when certain important celestial events will occur, such as the two equinoxes and solstices that correlate with spring, summer, autumn, and winter, etc.

Today, we hold that these correlations are merely astronomical in nature; but the imputing of meaning, for example, to the vernal equinox (which always corresponds to 0 degrees of the zodiac sign of Aries), is astrology pure and simple, in that we say that the vernal equinox means the end of winter and the onset of spring.

Whether or not additional celestial phenomena correlate with terrestrial events (geophysical, biological, or human-psychological) is merely a matter of accumulating enough statistical and qualitative data about them in order to decide either way. The data, however, must be accumulated before the decision is taken. The only real basic difference between today's astronomers and astrologers is that the former do not accumulate data about celestial-terrestrial correlations, while the latter do – and have done so since before 3000 B.C.

A novel way of thinking about the astronomer-astrologers of antiquity is that they were on a par with today's vividly scientific discipline comprised of cyclical analysis. Cycle researchers, to their surprise, can now statistically show that a very large number of terrestrial phenomena are timed in keeping with certain celestial events – especially cycles of growth and decline, upheaval and calm, war and peace, and long arid and wet climatic shifts. Cycle researchers, then, are capable of imputing meaning-correlations to celestial phenomena – and thus have become our new "astrologers," whether they like the appellation or not.

There is absolutely no reason at all to believe that the ancients were any less interested than contemporary people in the practical celestial-terrestrial matters reflected in our average desktop calendar. It is we who have to recover a broader range of celestial-terrestrial meaning-correlations, via cycles and astrological research, largely and only because modern astronomers turned their attention to outer space per se, and avoided interacting with correlative celestial-terrestrial events. These are the territory of astrology, whether it is called astrology or not.

When we regard our desktop calendars, we see them as 12 pages reflecting days, weeks, months, and the 365-day year. But behind this use of it, the calendar is based on the two equinoxes and solstices that divide the year into four equal 90-degree arcs of the zodiac. These four arcs refer to seasons, which are as important today as they were six millennia ago. And so it is the zodiac that we must examine – the centerpiece of astrology itself.

Although most dictionaries attribute the origin of the term "zodiac" to the late Greek *zodion* or *zodiakos*, difficulties are apparent in trying to establish the language to which it must have belonged. Phonetically speaking, the origin of the term can only minimally be considered as having been Greek.

In fact, since zodiacal representations are found preceding the rise of ancient Greek civilization, there is no reason to assume that either the astrological concept represented, or the term itself, is exclusively of Greek origin.

But there is a further mystery, and a very profound one. Wherever zodiac iconography is found, no matter what age or culture is involved, it always means the same thing. This is beyond any question. The iconography refers precisely to six to nine degrees on either side (above or below) of the ecliptic, through which the "wandering stars" (the planets, including the Sun and Moon) wobbled their way along the celestial sphere in repeating circular cycles. In contemporary terms, the zodiac might be called the planetary highway, or beltway.

Over time, all zodiac iconography consisted of from six to twelve representative figures (gods) portrayed against certain constellations, in a circular format, divided into (usually) 12 sections. In most, but not all, cultures, it is further subdivided into 360 degrees. The starting point of the circular zodiac is always the spring equinox in the northern hemisphere which, from some lost date in antiquity, has always been referred to as 0 degrees Aries.

Here, the first principal confusion about astrology is encountered. The astrologically uninitiated tend to understand that the zodiac is comprised of the famous 12 constellation arcs whose names are incorporated into it. This is not the case at all. The twelve signs are obviously named after the twelve constellations that once coincided with these arcs —when 0 degrees of Aries was indeed also the beginning point of the vernal equinox.

But, as many anti-astrological skeptics gleefully point out, the equinoxial beginning point has moved against the constellational background due to a longterm astronomical phenomenon called the Precession of the Equinoxial Point. This point slowly moves backward (over approximately 25,000 years) through the celestial constellations.

And so the actual astrological beginning point of the signs' influences is not derived from their background of stars and constellations, but from some conditions of momentum and gravitation, within the earth, by virtue of its annual revolution around the Sun; which is to say that the constellations are *not* the zodiac. The zodiac is based not upon astronomical factors per se, but upon certain consistencies having to do with seasonal changes on Earth.

The beginning, or starting point, of counting around the 360 degrees of the zodiacal beltway is always referred to as 0 degrees Aries, the beginning day of spring always known as the vernal equinox. The zodiac, then, is the "belt" of that part of the celestial sphere that encompasses the paths of all the planets (the "wandering stars" of the ancients) as they orbit the Sun, in relation to the vernal equinox, and not in relation to the constellations.

The center of the belt is the Sun's apparent orbit, called the "ecliptic" or the Sun's path, as it is seen geocentrically to move around the earth (or the orbit of Earth as it would be seen heliocentrically from the Sun). The zodiac belt extends 9 degrees above (north) and beneath (south) of the ecliptic, since the planets in their orbits incline and decline that much as they pursue their orbits.

Since at least the time of Hipparchus (2nd century A.D.), the greatest of the ancient astronomers, this belt has been divided into twelve 30-degree arcs, or signs, measured from the vernal equinox, and which altogether total 360 degrees. Here arises another somewhat confusing matter that so far has never been explained. The apparent motion of the Sun around the zodiac is actually Earth's motion through it.

But the zodiac time-terms are based on where the Sun is "at" at the vernal equinox (0 degrees Aries), at the summer solstice (0 degrees Cancer), at the autumnal equinox (0 degrees Libra), and at the winter solstice (0 degrees Capricorn). In zodiac "time" terms, the circular zodiac is divided equally into four 90-degree arcs as any circle would be, and is not apportioned according to the actual motion of the solar-Earth year.

The zodiac, then, is only secondarily based on the apparent daily motion of the Sun, and is principally "sensitive" to the great seasonal change-points that demark spring, summer, autumn, and winter. And, in fact, the great iconography or images of the signs of the zodiac are principally derived from the values and meanings of the four seasons, not from the apparent motion of the Sun against the celestial background.

Clearly, then, the zodiac is a function of the earth's inclination and gravitational motion, relative to the Sun, which also incorporates all the planets orbiting the Sun. It is not principally a function relative to the far-distant celestial constellations.

THE MEGALITHS

Archaeologists and investigators who specialize in researching megalithic monuments will already have realized that very many of them were constructed with special features to indicate the exact day of at least the vernal and autumnal equinoxes and the two solstices – the four principal points of any zodiac. Such megaliths are thus some kind of zodiacal-astrological monuments, and not merely astronomical-calendrical calculation edifices.

That this is adamantly the case can be understood very easily. If these same edifices were utilized to take note of the solar astronomical year, then their functions would quickly be "off" by five or six days – a discrepancy that would surely have been understood by the megalithic engineers who contrived the astonishing feats of heaving the gigantic megalithic monuments into place.

In this sense, then, more meaning was attributed to the tilting of Earth on its axis than to the solar year, which was five to six days longer then than now. The enormous megalithic edifices, then, are zodiacal ones, and anything zodiacal implies some form of astrological awareness and purpose beyond merely counting the astronomical days it takes to complete the (slightly longer) solar year.

Furthermore, to my knowledge, all of the known megalithic edifices are ringlike in form and dimension, and many of them are divided into sections radiantly, as is clearly the case of Stonehenge and Mount Pleasant Henge. The circularized construction at Newgrange is so exactly oriented to the zodiacal change-points as to accurately reflect them to this very day.

The zodiac, in any form, is the centerpiece not of astronomy, but of some kind of astrology that imputes meaning, and not only measurement, to factors having to do with Earth's axis tilt and resulting seasonal change-points. To continue to refer to such structures as "solar" or "calendrical" is to deny the mathematics and engineering involved in their construction.

The fact that these enormous edifices were constructed with data-meaning, not just calendrical counting, in mind is evidenced by the scope and massiveness of some of the megalithic monuments. Contrasted to these enormous monuments is the fact that Earth's maximum northern and southern tilt could, with trial and error, be determined by the shadows of two sticks placed upward in the ground about ten to twenty feet apart. The two shadows would coincide northward or southward exactly on only two days of the year: the two equinoxes.

Why render into monumental stone constructions, mounds, and pyramids what could more easily be determined by sticks in the ground? Well, Earth undergoes enormous geo-electromagnetic shifts at the four points of the equinoxes, and these have meaning to biological and psychological life. Those who favor a Greek etymological origin for "zodiac" link it to the term *zoon*, which, if difficult of translation, was associated in ancient Greece with the idea of "life" or with "living beings."

Indeed, the 12 different parts of the Greek zodiac pictured a series of beings which, like the Cherubim of Ezekiel, were held to "dwell" outside of time, with the limits of time being marked in the ancient cosmo-conception by the Sphere of Saturn. Geo- electromagnetic forces are certainly "outside" of time, as it is experienced in the human life cycle, and it is the zodiac "time" that reflects some sort of celestial-terrestrial, geo-electromagnetic, correlation-knowledge, whereas solar chronological time alone can reflect nothing of the kind.

I may be speaking out of my hat, but it is feasible to assume that the massiveness of the megalithic constructions was somehow commensurate with the important or ultra-important meanings implied by the massiveness. Megalithic edifices, such as Stonehenge, could not have been an easy undertaking – to say nothing of the Glastonbury Zodiac.

This particular zodiac consists of constructed mound-figures stretched over the Vale of Avalon in a great circle ten *miles* in diameter, the largest of the giant figures being five miles across. It portrays, in the correct order, the twelve signs of the zodiac, with a thirteenth lying outside of the circle, this being the "great dog of Langport," who guards the sacred abode of Annwn, just as Cerberus guarded the gates of Hades.

In ending, contemporary astrologers may be the first of the species that do not literally watch the heavens or the wandering stars moving in the zodiac beltway. Instead, myself included, we "watch" *ephemerides* and meanings printed in books, and even more recently, watch computer printouts of horoscopes and astro-statistics. Indeed, at many places on Earth today, the full splendor of the night skies is blotted out by artificial light and atmospheric pollution.

All megalithic and ancient astronomical-astrological structures, wherever they are found, were built in such ways that the celestial sphere could be watched from them. There would be a great difference between "watching," for example, a conjunction of Saturn and Jupiter from a chaotic natural surrounding, and watching one literally rising on what you know is the *exact* eastern horizon – from a spot imbued with ancient knowledge beyond your comprehension.

The former "watching" involves only the mind-intellect, but the latter easily could inspire deeper and fuller sensorium: prophetic, forecasting, or divinatory episodes that would clearly be of an inspired or "psychic" nature.

CHAPTER 2

ANCIENT EGYPTIAN ELECTRICIANS – IVAN SANDERSON – JULY 1969

A most disturbing new concept is arising to plague us. Concrete evidence of and for this is coming in at an increasing rate, and Forteans are just going to have to shift another gear, and fast, because for once, we show signs of being overridden both by the mystics and the scientists. Yet, if anything was strictly down, or up, our alley, it is this. The reasons for our having overlooked or deliberately ignored this development are, we believe, twofold.

First, Charles Fort died before the dawn of the modern technological age, so that those who took him as their starting point for their general interests were not confronted with it. Second, we feel that honest Forteans have been scared away from it due to its having for a long time been a particular pet of the mystics, including not a few religionists, and of the armies of kooks and crackpots – even unto the promoters of lost continents like Mu. The matter at issue is whether there was a worldwide technological civilization on this earth in extremely ancient times – before 4000 B.C.

The concept of ETIs (Extraterrestrial Intelligences) as they are now called (and even by such people as the scientists who worked on the benighted Condon Committee) visiting this planet throughout not just our historical period, but also since we evolved some two million years ago (and way back before that point in time to the very start of our Earth as a cosmic entity) is quite acceptable.

Even Dr. Carl Sagan, who is more or less the father of exobiology (the study of alien lifeforms), suggested just this as a possibility in his book *Intelligent Life In The Universe*. The research of Charles Hapgood into the origin of ancient maps (see his *Maps of the Ancient Sea Kings*) seems to prove, as nearly as anything can be proved, that some intelligences mapped the whole surface of the earth circa 20,000 B.C., using most refined spherical trigonometry, and probably did so, for the most part, from the air.

But the idea of mere humans running around laying coaxial cables, using computers, and building batteries circa 4000 B.C., just about when agriculture, writing, astronomy, and other simpler things are believed to have been "invented," is asking perhaps a little too much of pragmatists. But there are now very concrete evidences of such advanced technology, so that one is forced to ask the question: How?

There are dozens of suggestions but, as we see it, there is only one – as of our current state of knowledge – that is outstanding. This is that not only the basic enterprises like agriculture, medicine, writing, religion, law, and so forth, but also full-blown technologies were brought to this planet at the same time, and possibly by the same entities.

The best bet is that this took place just about 20,000 B.C., and that said entities first mapped the joint, then landed and started getting our Earth-evolved ancestors organized, by herding them into "Gardens of Eden" and so forth, and teaching a priesthood to govern them, by exercise of a limited knowledge of practical technology; but finally buzzed off again to look for more water planets. This they would appear to have done about 5000 B.C., either leaving us wholly on our own, or under the care of a few supervisors and our home-trained priests.

According to this notion, being virtually thrown on our own resources for the first time, we proceeded to make a monumental muck-up of everything, as is apparently our wont. The trouble may have been that then, just as now, we simply had not been sufficiently educated to cope even with the basics, let alone the residue of advanced technology.

This latter was left in the hands of the priesthoods, but they rapidly went all mystical and forgot how to make and run the essential machines, though some hung on for millennia and did not completely lose their minds, if not their grip. But a few of the basic things did take hold, like metallurgy; and it was this, more than anything else, that kept the remnants of the pre-ancient, ETI technology glimmering. A most puzzling and provocative example of a possible residue of this higher ETI technology is the famous Egyptian hieroglyphic of what looks like lightbulbs or electrical circuit.

This image appears in a book published in Sweden. The caption reads in Swedish (and we give this in the original, so that we may not be accused of mistranslation): "*Denna bild fran Dendera Templets sal 5 visar uppenbarligen elektriska lampor uppburna av hogspanningsisolatorer. Templet ar egentligen ett slags museum. Tekniken i Egypten stod vasentligt hogre fore den stora katastrofen an nagonsin senare.*"

There are several points of interest in this depiction. First, the Egyptians indicated rank by the size of the figures shown. Here the two main figures are very large in comparison to four in the background. They are also almost twice the size of the tailed baboon, holding a knife, standing behind what appears to be an altar. This is most unusual.

Thus, the two main figures must have been considered very important indeed, yet they have no regal appurtenances and are doing manual labor, even if they are high priests. But, of course, it is *what* they are bringing to this supposed altar that is of major interest. Nothing like this has been found elsewhere in Egypt.

Each appears to be bearing an object of very carefully composed form that seems to be transparent, since items that appear like snakes are shown within. These transparent constructions seem to be inserted into solid bases with some kind of circular, and perhaps threaded, closure at the end.

From each of these come what look like coaxial cables, which join and run into the little altar. Each main structure is apparently supported on a pedestal. These are somewhat but not entirely similar. Both have four flanges, but that on the left has two supporting arms extending from the second of these, and a small dome on its top.

There are those who have contended that these are an elaborate form of the sacred symbol known as the *ankh*, but frankly, they look much more like certain modern insulation fixtures for very high-tension power lines. What is more, the large transparent objects that the two big figures are carrying look almost too much like enormous "lightbulbs" containing heavy filaments.

Naturally, any Egyptologist who is asked to interpret this depiction will come up with a wild explanation, simply because one just cannot have priest-technicians or technician-priests wandering around in Egypt four thousand years ago installing high-tension cables with what one engineer suggested were some very clever male and female (i.e., positive and negative) terminals. Another engineer suggested they were television or radio tubes.

Meantime, however, Barney Nashold rolled in from Chicago. He and his wife have been on a Society For the Investigation of the Unexplained (SITU) expedition to Central America for the past year. When we showed him this frustrating business of the Egyptian "whatever-they-ares," he really flipped, because he has, over the years, accumulated a file of drawings taken from Nazean and other South American painted ceramics, which appear, on detailed analysis, to be formalized (and in part "allegorical") layouts for electronic circuitry.

This is a very interesting bit, and we will report upon it in considerable detail when Barney has had time to prepare his report with documentary evidence and analysis. Meantime, he requests that anyone among our ranks who might have been harboring similar suspicions and collecting supportive evidence get in touch with him via SITU. Any electronic engineers who enjoy working with puzzles might also like to lend a hand in this effort.

The results of our examination of the fresco from the Temple of Dendera, showing two figures holding objects on pedestals that look like giant lightbulbs, has become extremely complicated due to "extraneous" concerns. This was not unexpected, because a quarter of a century of experience has taught us that the average Fortean item, however tangible, is a pain in the neck to everybody but Forteans. Nonetheless, we did get somewhere in two departments.

The first is a proper translation of the caption under the illustration in Ivan Troenig's *Kulturer Fore Istide* ("Culture Before the Ice Age"), published by Nyloms, Uppsala, Sweden, in 1964. It reads: "This picture from Hall 5 of the Dendera Temple obviously shows electric lamps held up by high-tension insulators. The temple is actually a sort of museum. Technology in Egypt was considerably more advanced."

The text on the page opposite goes: "A variant of this symbolic vignette is found in the Egyptian Dendera Temple. This temple may be regarded as a museum, since objects of historical and technical interest were gathered together there. There are several reliefs (i.e., wall paintings) that without a doubt depict some type of enormous electric lamps, probably of an *urladdningstyp* nature – that is, some sort of construction similar to our (electrical) lamps."

(At least we have got this bit straight, but it ran us into the matter of this Temple of Dendera. This we will come back to in a moment.)

The best translation of *urladdningstyp* is "radio or TV discharging tube," the word "urladdning" meaning "discharging." Another piece of common sense that we have so far received is an assessment from one of our engineer members:

> Certain elements, especially the cables, are virtually an exact copy of engineering illustrations as currently used. The cable is shown as very heavy, and striated, indicating a bundle of many (multipurpose) conductors, rather than a single high-voltage cable.

> As a matter of fact, a single (high-voltage) cable would be much thinner. If the insulation was required to be that heavy for extreme high voltages, or moderately high voltages at high currents, rest assured that no technician would be holding the associated device. Coronal leakage would "get" him most swiftly. The supporting stands would have to be much taller

and heavier to withstand such voltages.

It is much more likely that the cable is, as stated, a multipurpose conductor, wrapped and insulated with an outer jacket. If this were a lightbulb, the maximum size of both would be explainable by heavy current demands; but megavoltage insulators of such large size would not be required.

It would seem to follow that moderately high voltages are in use; a connector is obviously employed; some type of supporting base-to-glass seal seems apparent. However, the two "bulbs" are not identical, as shown by the designs on their sides and on the base stands.

I do not think that they are transparent, as the technician's body is not visible through the device; it would seem more obvious that these are identifying markings, or codings (as a type number on a TV camera tube), probably indicating use of the device.

Since the cables seem to originate at the altar, one wonders if this is a manually controlled setup, or remotely controlled. Further, with both devices set at an angle, and shown aimed at the wall, could they not be the ancient equivalent of the modern TV projection system?

One should also note that the two technicians, especially the one on the left, seem to be wearing a mask device, or eye shield. Unless the drawing is badly reproduced, both have some type of apparatus in their ears, suggesting the equivalent of modern TV cameramen, complete with radio receiver and/or earphones for direct instruction during a "show."

Engineers are wonderful, especially when they contemplate matters outside their strict regimen. There was a rider to the above that stated:

It should be noted in passing that the priesthoods of old were masters at "putting on a show" to impress the local natives. And what could be more convincing of their "magical" abilities than a mysteriously appearing (and disappearing) image on a temple wall? After all, the best way to impress the natives is to scare them half to death.

The replies so far received from the archaeologists and historians, and notably Egyptologists, have been in marked contrast to these pragmatic comments. Several to whom we applied have not even answered. One said he could not translate the hieroglyphs shown in the depiction, and another said he would not! When it came to the business of trying to identify the Temple of Dendera, we ran into some pretty obvious chicanery.

Everybody seems to transliterate Ancient Egyptian names in their own ways; we have Denduras, Dendaras, Dhenduras, and so on. But the most popular form of our temple among these savants seems to be the little one-room temple of Dendur, which has now been acquired by the Metropolitan Museum of New York and is apparently being re-erected under a special dome in New York's Central Park.

This is, of course, the safest path to follow, because it has only one hall, and *no such depiction in it*. So devious, in fact, have been the responses of the Egyptologists that we have applied directly to Egypt. So once again, we must ask you to wait.

INSTANT EVERYTHING – JANUARY 1970

In the book *Chariots of the Gods* by Erich von Däniken, there is an interesting paragraph.

> Today, science reaches many of its goals with seven-league boots. It took 112 years for photography to develop to the stage of a clear picture. The telephone was ready for use in 56 years, and only 35 years of scientific research were needed to develop radio to the point of perfect reception. But the perfecting of radar took only 15 years. The stages of epoch-making discoveries and developments are getting shorter and shorter; black and white television was on view after 12 years of research, and the construction of the first atom bomb took a mere 6 years. These are a few examples from 50 years of technical progress.

This presents a rather eerie prospect, especially if we do a little interpolating as well as extrapolating. First, let us go back a piece. It apparently took several million years to produce a human being. It took these creatures at least a million years to institute an industry (i.e., the regular creation of wood, bone, horn, and stone tools). Then, several hundred thousand more years were needed before these creatures stumbled across metals, metallurgy, and true industry.

That appears to have been some ten thousand years ago, but humans then struggled along with copper, gold, silver, tin, and bronze for a long time before they got to iron, and it was only 200 years ago that the basis of modern technology (i.e., steel) was developed. If you put this lot on a graph below von Däniken's examples, you will note the fact that such major developments form an almost perfect geometrical progression. So let us turn the coin and do a little extrapolating.

You can keep dividing time forever and still never get to zero, but by the time you get this graph uncoiled to the point where it appears to go straight up (i.e., to the Einsteinian speed of light), you will have virtually instant discovery. What a Fortean must then needs ask is: what happens next?

Does enquiry and development come to a stop, or do we break the time barrier and start developing things before they are developed? Or alternatively, do we develop things before they have been planned or conceived? There being no such thing as the present, are we confined within certain limits, or can we jump this theoretical barrier and predict? Could this be an opening wedge into the whole field of prediction and precognition?

The greatest confrontation coming up today is between two parties of pragmatists, not between pragmatists and mystics. This dialogue will absorb an increasing amount of time and thought on the part of all pragmatists and especially scientists, because concrete (i.e., tangible), recordable, and reproducible proof of a number of intangibles is now turning up.

The best example of this may be found in Walter McGraw's book *The World of the Paranormal*. The essential point that everybody has to appreciate is that by the use of new physical machinery, electronic and otherwise, we are now beginning to be able to obtain proof of at least some of the mental and other intangible processes that manifestly control not only life as we know it, but also the entire universe and existence itself.

In fact, we are taking the "E" out of "ESP" and replacing it with the much more realistic "S" for "super" (or supra, if you will). In other words, there is nothing spiritual, mystical, or even occult (meaning "hidden") about the amazing actions and reactions of man and other animals and plants.

The list of man's senses passed the 25 mark long ago, and every day, more are being added (although we don't know yet what physical parts of our body constitute the mechanism of their operation). The sensory proclivities, and both for sending as well as receiving, of other animals are positively overwhelming in their multiplicity.

Take, for instance, the fact that almost a dozen "sense organs" have been found (as physical structures) on the bottom segment of the antenna of one small fly; and we don't know what any of them are for!

Another essential point to bear in mind is one for the technologists. This is that the electromagnetic is not the only energy band in our cosmos. How many others there may be remains to be discovered, but there is definitely one of immense capability upon which our "mental waves" operate.

Moreover, nothing that we know of in the EM band has so far been demonstrated to interfere with this "mental" band. Nor can we detect the mental band through the EM band. And just because there now appears to be some evidence of a "G" (gravity) band, for goodness sakes, lot us not jump to the conclusion that thought runs on gravity.

[Editor's note: As of 2017, no one has successfully proven that gravity is separate from electromagnetism, so the jury is still out on whether gravity is fueling our thoughts. It probably is, although exactly how it may be interacting with light to do so is still unknown.]

LITTLE GOLD AIRPLANES A THOUSAND YEARS OLD – APRIL 1970

This fascinating item got kind of lost in the shuffle due to its having been asked for as an article by *Argosy* magazine. At the risk of being heavily censured by that publication's editors, we are constrained to observe that the article they produced was lousy, and for the following reasons.

First, the photos reproduced did not display the essential points; second, those that they did publish were not only irrelevant but misleading; third, not one of the photos or drawings mentioned in the text were reproduced – most notably, the object was seen from the side (with lettering on upright tailfins), which nullified the strongest arguments for the thesis developed by aeronautical engineers to explain these remarkable little objects.

We now have to add to this the fact that a great deal more has been learned about these items since the publication of that article. No less than half a dozen more little gold pieces of similar design have turned up all over the place, such as in the Chicago Natural History Museum and in the Smithsonian Institution. The whole business has, as a result, become greatly more important.

About two-dozen of these items, in several collections, appear to display a progressive development from, and/or deterioration of, the original models, which are fairly simple and straightforward. These become ever more elaborately ornamented and fantastic. Interestingly, they do not become more naturalistic (as they should if later artists and artisans, working from the early plane-like models, had tried to convert them into the form of known animals, which they knew so well and modeled so precisely).

To the contrary, they become ever more fantastic, showing, we tend to believe, that they knew the original things from which they made; their models were not animals, but inanimate things that we would call "out of this world."

It is interesting to note also that our first article, mentioned above, hardly caused a ripple among the reading public. This puzzled many at first, but then it was pointed out that the age of these artifacts had hardly been mentioned and not stressed. And there came then a rather startling discovery. This may sound obnoxious to many when stated flatly. It is simply that a very high percentage of the public today, and notably the younger generations in countries like the U.S., labor under the most extraordinary delusions about history.

For instance, the notion that Henry Ford invented the automobile is almost universal, just as is the belief that Edison invented electric light, and that just about every other currently used technological development like TV, radar, and radio telescopes were first invented in the United States.

But more alarming is the discovery made recently that youngsters, brought up on media techniques as everyday facts of their lives, have absolutely no concept of their historical background or age. Even a high school science teacher on a television show, competing for a thousand dollars, gave the answer 1770 A.D. as the year that the Atlantic was first crossed by radio!

As a result of this appalling ignorance (which is not their fault, but that of our so-called educational system and TV for the most part), the idea that some South American Indian artists were making little gold models of swept-wing jet planes a thousand years ago means nothing to them. The general attitude, we personally discovered, was a sort of "so what?" This was often followed up with: "Anyhow, what's so great about that?"

The "discovery" of these little artifacts is probably one of the most pertinent ever made through archaeological enterprise – if it is a true discovery – and it has become much more pertinent since more of these items have come to light and the aerodynamics engineers and designers have had a chance to analyze them.

The original notion that they were "zoomorphic fantasies," which was nothing more than a last-ditch, desperate resort on the part of archaeologists and historians faced with such an alarming mystery, has now been completely demolished by the zoologists who, with all the will in the world (and they would love to be able to confirm their colleagues in this), simply cannot come up with any animal that has the features of these items.

Since so many of those features are exactly and precisely those of airplanes, at least a possibility was therefore to be faced: namely, that somebody had airplanes circa 500 to 800 A.D. in northwestern South America, and that local artists made models of them to the best of their ability.

The question as to who made the things that formed the models for these little pendants, presents quite another problem. There are three alternatives. Either 1) there was a highly developed human civilization at that time, or earlier; 2) these things came out of the sea and were devices built by some underwater civilization; or 3) they came down out of the skies from space, and were subsidiary craft employed by intelligent entities from elsewhere visiting, surveying, or colonizing this planet.

[Editor's note: Another possibility is that at least one artisan saw into the future, perhaps while under the influence of hallucinogenic herbs, and made a model of what he or she saw. Still, this doesn't explain why subsequent artisans treated the original as an "inanimate" object, unless the first artisan clearly saw that planes of the future were machines and not animals.]

WERE EGYPTIANS FIRST IN AUSTRALIA? – JANUARY 1971

This was the headline on a short piece from *The London Sunday Express*, sent to us by SITU member No. 162. It was datelined Sydney, and read as follows:

> Did Ancient Egyptians surf at Bondi, a suburb of Sydney? Historian Rex Gilroy plans to lead an expedition into central Australia to prove that Egyptians and other races found Australia thousands of years before Captain Cook. He believes he already has evidence that Arab *dhows* explored the New South Wales coast about 3,500 B.C.

> He is studying a collection of bronze plates, coins, pottery, and hieroglyphics found near Bondi and other parts of Australia. Now he will search for huge reliefs of Egyptian deities reported to have been found by Aboriginals on a cliff face in central Australia.

> "These discoveries could rewrite the history of Australia," said Mr. Gilroy, director of the Mount York Natural History Museum. "Evidence of the landings of Egyptians, including Aboriginal carvings of their dhows and clothing, is coming to light all the time."

This is intriguing, though one wonders which Arabs they are talking about.

Had Mr. Gilroy said "Phoenicians," it would seem more likely. Also, the Egyptians were not notoriously good sailors, despite Thor Heyerdahl's latest success. Bear in mind that Ra I and Ra II were built not by Egyptians, but by imported Bolivian Indians! Nevertheless, we pursued Mr. Gilroy.

Our own reference works having failed us, we called the Australian News and Information Bureau. They had heard nothing of it, and were no more successful in finding a town called Mount York than we had been; nor were they able to find any reference to Mr. Rex Gilroy. We then wrote to the Foreign Editor of *The Sunday Express*, who very kindly checked with his correspondent in Sydney, and sent us an address for Mr. Gilroy.

In the meantime, we had also written to the Australian Museum in Sydney to ask their help. And we got it, in the form of one of the most refreshingly frank letters we have ever seen, which came from Elizabeth Pope, their acting director. And we quote:

> I have your letter of 14th September 1970, addressed to the Director of the Australian Museum. Dr. Talbot, our director, is at present overseas, but in his absence, I think I can completely answer the request made in your letter about Mr. Rex Gilroy, self-styled director of the Mount York Natural History Museum.
>
> Without being too strong, I think I can state that you can completely disregard any claims as to discoveries, either of a natural history nature or archaeological, made by Mr. Gilroy. We have already notified all the responsible newspapers in Australia that they should disregard any claims he makes. His work is bogus and he is possibly slightly deranged.
>
> He has a small private museum situated in the Blue Mountains of New South Wales near Mount York (nearest large town: Katoomba). We have had trouble with him in connection with fossils, with this particular claim that he has found traces of Arabs and Egyptians in Australia, and on many other occasions.
>
> He makes wild statements to small local newssheets, which publish them as "sensational findings," and then these get extracted into large city dailies in Australian States. If you want some details as to his "craziness," I would suggest that you communicate with our curator of paleontology, Dr. Alex Ritchie. I repeat you can completely disregard any claims of Gilroy in this matter.

It would be rather fun to have Egyptians and Arabs in Australia, but it seems clear that Mr. Gilroy has a bee in his bonnet. We would like to know more about the alleged "bronze plates, coins, pottery, and hieroglyphics" mentioned, and in fact, had written to him before receiving Miss Pope's reply to our enquiry. But Mr. Gilroy has not answered.

There are some very curious and fully authenticated Aboriginal paintings of people who bear no resemblance to any Australian Aborigine; they don't resemble any Arab or Egyptian, either. And, despite the fact that we have a tendency to be very cautious in accepting flat statements by orthodox scientists, the comments on Gilroy's general reputation indicate that anything he offers should be fully backed with facts and artifacts.

RED-HAIRED PEOPLE-EATERS

Scores of redheaded mummies, averaging 6-1/2 to 7 feet tall, and thousands of artifacts have been taken from a smoke-coated, exceptionally dry cave some 22 miles southwest of Lovelock, Nevada. Paiute Indians living in Lovelock state matter-of-factly that these were cannibals who preyed on the Paiutes and were eventually exterminated by them. The last remnants of the cannibal tribe holed up in this cave, and were suffocated by enormous fires built at the entrance.

Annie Bill, 68, a Paiute and a lifelong resident of Lovelock, said, "All members of the tribe who were exterminated had red hair. I have some of their hair, which has been handed down from father to son. I have a dress, which has been in our family a great many years, trimmed with this reddish hair. Old Paiutes always called the redheads 'Siwash' Indians, but many of my people really wondered if the redheads were Indians at all."

Her grandparents told her that their grandparents described the cannibals as having long faces and light skin "like white man." This may seem a rather remote source of information, but nonliterate peoples often do transmit their tribal history from generation to generation with remarkable fidelity.

The anthropologists and archaeologists are rather rude about the story of cannibalism and red hair, claiming that the color of the hair was due to "age or chemical action." And Donald R. Tuohy, curator of anthropology at the Nevada State Museum, has announced, apparently with some heat, that the Paiute stories are "myths – pure and simple fabrications." He further "believes" that the Paiutes knew of the existence of the cave and its contents long before its discovery by white men in 1912, and concocted this story to explain it.

He is quite right on one count. Sarah Winnemucca Hopkins, daughter of the Paiute chief, Old Winnemucca, published a book entitled Life Among the Paiutes in 1883, in which she gives the whole story and states that the last of the cannibals were exterminated by her people earlier in the 19th century.

Recent carbon-14 dating tests indicate that the cave was occupied as late as 1800-1850, which certainly supports her story; and no one has even tried to suggest that this late occupation was by the Paiutes, who were not cave dwellers.

The question of who these cannibals were, and where they came from, is still unresolved. The earliest occupation of the cave is dated as somewhere between 2000 and 3000 B.C., but it was not occupied continuously up to 1800. Most of the artifacts are what one would expect: baskets, nets, duck decoys, arrowheads, and the like.

But one artifact is most unusual. Preserved at Stoker's Museum in Winnemucca, this is a calendar stone marked with 52 dots on the inside and 365 dots on the outside.

Clarence (Pike) Stoker, curator (and presumably owner) of the museum, has speculated that if the redheads weren't Amerindians, then "it's very possible they were descendants of Egyptians who sailed to America hundreds of years ago." But red hair suggests Phoenicians rather than Egyptians. Phoenicians do seem to have gotten around, but that they were all giants and indulged in cannibalism is questionable.

Current studies of the artifacts, mummies, and some 5000 human coprolites (fossilized excrement) may provide an answer to this conundrum. In the meantime, we think it impolite to call the Paiutes liars, and unwise to lean too heavily on Thor Heyerdahl's Egyptian exercises.

"THEY ALL DISCOVERED AMERICA"

The most startling pronouncement in the field of archaeology last year was undoubtedly Professor Cyrus H. Gordon's considered pronouncement that some Mediterranean people, probably including at least some Hebrews, got to this continent 1000 or more years before Columbus.

Dr. Gordon stated for the record that a tribal group of indigenes called the Melungeons offer clear evidence of this fact, not only in their legends, but also in their physical appearance. An inscribed stone was unearthed from one of their burial mounds in Tennessee, in 1885, by one Cyrus Thomas, who was working with the Smithsonian.

Gordon further stated that "this group of people are neither Amerindian nor Negro, and are Caucasian, but not Anglo-Saxon." The stone was found under one of nine skeletons in the mound. "The archaeological circumstances of the discovery," Dr. Gordon said, "rule out any chance of fraud or forgery, and the inscription attests to a migration of Jews."

It was brought to his attention by Dr. Joseph D. Mahan, Jr. of the Columbus, Georgia Museum of Arts and Crafts. It has been lying in the Smithsonian since its discovery, but ignored because the inscription was initially read upside down and made no sense.

It bears eleven characters, including five letters that Dr. Gordon read as "For the Land of Judah," in a style of writing used in Canaan around the beginning of this millennium. He suggests that they were inscribed about the time when "Jews migrated here to escape the long hand of Rome after the disastrous Jewish defeats in 70 to 135 A.D." He adds that the Melungeons are descendants of Mediterranean people, who themselves believe that they came to the New World in ships about 2000 years ago.

This is but another nail in the coffin of the "Ocean Blue in 1492" and all that "discovery" nonsense, and a cornerstone in the ever-growing edifice of Near Eastern exploration of, and settlement in, the New World, starting 2000 years before that episode. It was Dr. Gordon, moreover, who jolted us two years ago by pronouncing another inscribed stone slab found in the Amazon Basin as being of Phoenician origin.

Before that we have the massive work of Prof. Ramos, bringing to light dozens of other petroglyphs, including perfect fish and Indian rhinoceroses filled with Aramaic-type Phoenician letters in the same country. Add to these the coins found in the bottoms of wells all down the eastern coastal plain of North America, tombs in South America, and statuettes of bearded men with Caucasian features in Central America, and the Columbus buffs begin to look a bit silly.

(Columbus was accused by his captains of not being able to read the maps given to him by his brother. I wish I had had some maps when I "discovered" a new mountain in Africa; it would have saved me a lot of time, trouble, and expense.)

A point of interest may be worthy of addition to this matter. It is not generally realized that not all the Hebrew tribes of old were landlubbers. Several groups broke away from the God Yahweh and followed Baal of the Phoenicians. The Palestinian coastal strip became home to sea people, like the Philistines, and the subjects of the ancient sea kings.

They nonetheless remained Hebrews (the term "Jewish" is only a religious designation), and they were still around at the time of Columbus, usually as the specsioneers (or pursers) on ships of almost all nations, handling trading and financial matters.

There is the fascinating story of the specsioneer on Cortez' flagship, who was a Hebrew and who, upon seeing the first ocellated turkeys, named them *tokhe'* in Hebrew, since their spread tails displayed eyes on them, like the tails of peacocks – a bird he alone knew. (Incidentally our turkey was taken to Spain, but developed in Holland and Belgium, and then the Spanish Low Countries. It did not spread to Turkey until very modern times!)

There is massive evidence that the crews of trading vessels from the eastern Mediterranean were always extremely mixed, and that not only the coastal Hebrews, but even the inland tribesmen, did an awful lot of boating. Hebrews, and notably Sephardim, settled in earliest times at the terminals of sea-lanes everywhere, and apparently of ocean lanes as well. They were the brokers and the first maritime insurance agents. If the Phoenicians got to the New World, Hebrews undoubtedly arrived with them.

MORE ON MERCURY ENGINES – JULY 1972

Through the courtesy of our Advisor for Cultural Anthropology and Linguistics, Professor Roger W. Wescott, of Drew University, we have received the following most valuable further information on the ancient Indian vimanas (flying saucers), and the first fully documented translation of a reliable Sanskrit text published by a recognized scholar.

All the texts that we have had in the past have been pronounced to be "shoddy" by the scholars to whom we submitted them for translation. Also, in this new extract, the much more vital matter of the mercury engines crops up again.

Said extracts are from *Yantras or Mechanical Contrivances in Ancient India* by V. Raghavan, published in 1956, and go as follows:

> The *Samaranganasutradhara* ascribed to Bhoja is, in many ways, a rare treatise in Sanskrit literature; besides the *Arthasastra*, it is the only theoretical text that has substantial information on our subject. Its value, however, is greater than that of the Arthasastra, as Bhoja goes into the details of the construction of these yantras, and explains at the beginning the principles underlying yantras.

The most curious of the yantras described by Bhoja in this chapter is, of course, the one that rises and travels in the air. From the previous notices of this aerial machine, only the barest details of its makeup could be gleaned. The only text that gives us some knowledge of its actual construction is this work of Bhoja.

Firstly, Bhoja mentions the main material of its body as light wood, laghu-daru. Its shape is that of a huge bird, mahavinhanga, with a wing on each side. The motive force is then explained. In the bowels of the structure is to be a fire-chamber with mercury placed over a flame. The power generated by the heated mercury, helped by the concurrent action of the wings, which are flapped by a rider inside, makes the yantra go up and travel far.

A heavier Daru-vimana is then described. It contains, not one as in the previous case, but four pitchers of mercury over iron ovens. The boiling mercury ovens produce a terrific noise, which is put to use in battle to scare away elephants. By strengthening the mercury chambers, the roar could be increased, so that by it, elephants are thrown completely out of control. This specific military use of aircraft against elephants tempts one to suggest that the Hasti-yantra (advocated by Kautilya against elephants) was something like the heavier Daru-vimana described by Bhoja.

There may be some lacunae in the description. Bhoja does not fail to mention that some vital knowledge is kept back as a secret, an idea which we noticed in the Brihatkatha story also. It is, however, clear that mercury vapor ought not to be confused as providing any lifting power. It was evidently converted into mechanical power, and the machine must have risen by the flapping of the wings, and further movement must have been due to the manipulation of the wings and the flow of air itself, on the analogy of the flight of birds.

This may come as somewhat of a depressant to the flying saucer buffs, since they seem to have gained the impression that the vimanas were wingless craft that could fly not only over a bunch of elephants, but also all over the world and out into space. The flapping wings as a means of gaining lift will be a disappointment to the engineers and probably provoke wry smiles among them, to say the least.

But to a whole new breed of scholars that has only recently arisen, it is going to give much cheer and impetus to their various studies. These are the historians of technology, who are working out of a dozen cultural centers scattered all over the world now, all of whom are bringing to light an increasing flow of actual (tangible) artifacts that are either themselves technical devices, or scale models of such – all the way from selenial calendars from the late Paleolithic to various aeroforms between 500 B.C. and 500 A.D.

That the Ancients did have a knowledge of flight can no longer be denied. However, the Indians alone offer us concrete written information on power sources for them. The Near Eastern items would appear to be gliders or sailplanes, though one Roman blandly states that he made his model "fly by compressed air." (Who, I ask, was compressing air in 200 A.D.?)

The South American types probably would not fly without power, but we are having copies of these tested in a NASA wind tunnel because, if they can do so, we will have one of the greatest breakthroughs in aerodynamics yet. The Ancient Egyptian item is the most exciting and confusing of all because, while it has the conformity of a glider, its fuselage looks more like a heavy-lift cargo plane we now have on the drawing boards (but which is still full of bugs).

However, here we are more interested in the "engines" that are alleged to have activated these aerial machines. In *Science* magazine (3rd January 1969), two scientists, Gerald Schubert and J.A. Whitehead, described a remarkable discovery that they had made about heating mercury. On filling a wide, shallow, circular dish of mercury and then revolving a naked flame around and around under said dish, they observed that the mercury began to revolve in a contrary direction and with increasing velocity. So far we have been unable to find anything further published on this or any subsequent experiments, but will be applying directly to Messrs. Schubert and Whitehead.

Did all the noise come from the mercury, or from the machinery it drove? We must assume that this was part of the "secret," and so we shall never know, unless somebody with an eye to this mystery spots something in a text by a renegade technician. The Indian princes seem to have maintained whole stables of such purely practical working technicians and, presumably, labs for them to work in. A few writings by such have been found, giving rather intimate details of other "machinery."

If they had flying machines, did they invent them and their power sources themselves, or is this still another hint that there was once a much older and even more advanced, worldwide civilization that left a residue of its knowledge with native priesthoods?

Now that we know somebody was mining iron ore in 40,000 B.C., it looks more and more as if this were so; and, be it noted, the first of the metals to corrode is steel, and the last gold. As we dig down, we find ultimately only gold copies but, strangely, they are the most competently made and of the most advanced items – so advanced that archaeologists have either so far overlooked them for what they are, or have deliberately set them aside.

"YESU" OF THE DRUIDS – JANUARY 1973

Throughout recorded history, there has been a legend in the southwest peninsula (Somerset and Cornwall) of England and southern Ireland that the Palestinian Essene whom we call "Jesus Christ" visited and resided at a place, today called Glastonbury, in northern Somerset. This is a matter of enormous historical interest, and not only to theologians. Just look it up in any encyclopedia.

Let us, however, leave the theological aspects of this out of the picture for the moment, and concentrate on the historical, with some reference to botanical matters: first, the matter of the flowering thorn tree, which is really the basis for this whole legend.

In Glastonbury, County of Somerset, England, and only there in all of western Europe, is there found a thorn bush which flowers twice a year, and almost exactly on Christmas and the Christian Easter.

The story goes that these bushes in that area are all descended from a staff left outside a hut, during one of his periodic visits to the tin mines of Britain, by one Joseph of Arimathea, a prominent Hebraic and Roman official, who was also the uncle of Christ and his guardian.

The so-called "thorn trees" constitute the genus *Crataegus* (a member of the *Rosaceae* family), of which there are at least 150 full species and now over 900 subspecies, though most of the latter were developed in North America. The common species of Britain is *Crataegus oxyacantha*, of which there are also numerous very distinct natural sub-species. They are all shrubs or small trees with, occasionally, an old giant up to 45 feet.

The original indigenous distribution of this species was apparently from northwestern Europe, north to 62-1/2' latitude in Sweden; and then east, via the sub-boreal belt, all the way to farthest Siberia; and then back west again, north of the mountains to Asia Minor and North Africa. However, there is another species known as *C. praecox* that flowers twice a year, and which is indigenous to the eastern Mediterranean, and thence east, south of the distribution of the *C. oxyacantha* group.

So why is there only one tiny place in Western Europe where this species has become implanted; and why should seeds taken from it there (crossbred or otherwise) fail to perform?

Next, there can in no way be any doubt that the Phoenicians and other Palestinians obtained a major part of their supply of tin and other metals from this area in the islands that the Greeks called the Cassiterides. Therefore, who would wish to deny that a leading metal trader, such as this Joseph of Arimathea, should have taken his adopted son, age 12, on a trip with him to the west?

As to whether or nor this adopted son happened to be the man we know (historically) as Jesus Christ is of no concern to us at the moment; but, since that person appears to have been missing from Palestine from the age of 12 until 30, there is no reason to suppose that it was not he.

It has been suggested by Colin Renfrew that the most ancient monotheistic theological influences spread not from the eastern Mediterranean to the north and west, but from the north and west *to* the south and east. In other words, the late Neolithic and especially the Celtic ecclesiastics (often erroneously call the "Druids") were the first monotheists.

A Celtic priest could probably teach a Palestinian Essene (more than could any other people whom he could reach) a pure philosophy that he could develop to apply to his "ministry" when he went home. The fascinating thing is that the Celts did have a Messiah belief, and this great philosopher and teacher-to-be was called "Yesu." Coincidence?

For now, we would just like to revive this fascinating legend, and introduce it to the people of the United States.

How many of you "exported" Celts have observations to make on this? Try an encyclopedia first; then see if you have any "ancestors" still alive; re-read the Bible; and then bombard your stunned neighbors. There's more to this legend than meets the eye.

GIANT SKELETONS – JULY 1973

We would not care to even try to guess how many chaps are barging around the country "hunting" a Sasquatch or Bigfoot, but we have a suggestion for them: Try tracking down some of the many giant skeletons reported from all over the place.

A recent article in *The Winnipeg Free Press* tells of the successful search for a fossil whale skeleton originally found by a farmer in 1906. In 1963, a local historian mentioned this in a book, and Richard Harrington, curator of quaternary zoology at Canada's National Museum of Natural Sciences, spent a year tracking it down through old records. It was found in a hayloft.

The North Jersey Highlander (Spring 1973 issue) includes an article by the editor, W. Mead Stapler, entitled "A Mystery in History." It concerns giant skeletons. Mr. Stapler notes that *The Conservationist* (for December-January 1966-67), a publication of the New York State Department of Environmental Conservation in Albany, published a piece on "The Lesser Wilderness-Tug Hill" area north of Utica, in which the author discussed the finding of "skeletons of giants, with double rows of teeth in each jaw."

In *The History of Bedford, Somerset, and Fulton Hopkins, Counties in Pennsylvania* by Waterman and Hopkins is described the finding of the "remains" of a people of "gigantic size" who preceded the Iroquois in an area about 100 miles south of Tug Hill, and were called the Allegwi by the Iroquois. In Benjamin J. Lossing's *Field Book of the Revolution*, there is a footnote:

> I saw, in the possession of Mr. Neilson, many relics plowed up from the battlefield at Saratoga, such as cannonballs, grapeshot, tomahawks, arrowheads, buttons, knives, etc., and among them were some teeth, evidently front ones, but double.

The teeth were attributed to the Hessians, but undoubtedly this is simply the result of propaganda.

The New York Times of December 2, 1930 states:

> Discovery of apparent remains of a race of giants has been made at Sayopa, Sonora, a mining town 300 miles south of the Mexican border. J.E. Coker, a mining engineer, reports that laborers clearing ranchland near the Yaqui River dug into an old cemetery where bodies of men, averaging eight feet in height, were found buried tier on tier.

The claim was dismissed by Bernard Brown, curator of the American Museum of Natural History, as pure exaggeration. As usual, there is no indication that he saw the skeletons.
Here is another entry from *The New York Times*, dated the 14th of February 1936:

> Managua, Nicaragua – Press accounts say that the skeleton of a gigantic man, with head missing, has been unearthed at El Boquin, on the Mico River, in the Chontales district. The

ribs are a yard long and four inches wide, and the shinbone is too heavy for one man to carry. "Chontales" is an Indian word meaning "wild men."

The New York Times of June 9, 1936 had this to say:

> Miami, Florida – A tale of human skeletons eight feet long, embedded in the sand of an uninhabited little island off Southern Florida was brought here today by three fishermen. They exhibited a piece of one skull containing six teeth.
>
> E.M. Miller, zoologist at the University of Miami, said the mandible was that of a man, and was probably several hundred years old. "It is entirely probable that this find might be important," he commented. The men said that the skulls were unusually thick, the jaws protruded, and the eye sockets were high in the head.

And then there are the Native Americans with horns, as reported by Robert R. Lyman in his book, *Forbidden Land*:

> Eight hundred and more years ago, giant Indians with horns roamed the Black Forest of Pennsylvania beneath giant trees.
>
> At Tioga Point, on the Murray farm, a short distance from Sayre, in Bradford County, an amazing discovery was made. Dr. G.P. Donehoo, State Historian and a former minister of the Presbyterian Church in Coudersport, together with Prof. A.B. Skinner of the American Investigating Museum, and Prof. W.K. Morehead of Phillips Andover Academy, uncovered an Indian mound. They found the bones of 68 men that were believed to have been buried about the year 1200 A.D.
>
> The average height of these men was 7 feet, while many were much taller. On some of the skulls, two inches above the perfectly formed forehead, were protuberances of bone, evidently horns that had been there since birth. Some of the specimens were sent to the American Investigating Museum.
>
> We have more evidence that very tall men once lived in the Black Forest. In December 1886, W.H. Scoville of Andrews Settlement discovered an Indian mound at Ellisburg. When opened, the skeleton of a man was found. It was close to eight feet in length. Trees on and around the mound indicated that burial had been made at least 200 years before.

These are only a few of the reports of giant skeletons that have been found, and in many cases, said to have been sent to local museums. Writing to museums or even puttering about in their basements may not be as "exciting" as tramping through the woods, but it is likely to be far more productive.

Quite a few Mothman and Bigfoot hunters have told us that they spent time "in the field" and saw nothing, but very often had the feeling that they were being watched. In fact, one group was told by a forest ranger that he had seen a Sasquatch trailing them! They came home empty-handed. Skeletons in museums or barn lofts won't run away, but they must be searched out.

Local museums are more likely to have specimens "buried" in their collections than the big institutions – particularly those operated by orthodox scientists who do not want to have to rewrite their textbooks. Troublesome items are prone to lose their labels, and unlabeled items are of no value, and are therefore thrown out. Small museums, in many cases connected with a local historical society, often depend on part-time volunteer help –but such persons are usually very knowledgeable.

THE CHINESE PYRAMID – OCTOBER 1973

One of the tantalizing stories we have been working on is that of an enormous pyramid in China, far exceeding in size any in Egypt or elsewhere. Ron Dobbins has found for us several of the "initial" reports in *The New York Times*, and a photograph of a pyramid from a book published in 1902. *The New York Times* article, in a UPI dispatch datelined Shanghai, March 27, 1947, reads in part:

> A giant pyramid in the isolated mountains of Shensi Province, in western China, was reported today by Col. Maurice Sheahan, Far Eastern director for Trans World Airline (TWA).
>
> From the air, Colonel Sheahan said, the pyramid seems to dwarf those of Egypt. He estimated its height at 1,000 feet, and its width at the base at 1,500 feet.
>
> The pyramid, he said, is at the foot of the Tsinling Mountains, about forty miles southwest of Sian, capital of the province. A second pyramid, he continued, appears much smaller.
>
> The pyramid, Colonel Sheahan went on, is at the far end of a long valley, in an inaccessible part. At the near end, he said, are hundreds of small burial mounds. These can be seen, he said,

from the Lung-Hai railroad.

"When I first flew over it, I was impressed by its perfect pyramidal form and its great size." Colonel Sheahan said. "I did not give it thought during the war years, partly because it seemed incredible that anything so large could be unknown to the world. From the air, we could see only small footpaths leading to a village at the site of the pyramid."

China said that because of the almost complete absence of communications, or even trails, in some parts of the West China mountains, it was not impossible that a huge pyramid might have been long forgotten.

The article goes on to note that Dr. James L. Clark of the American Museum of Natural History and Dr. Arthur Upham Pope of the Asia Institute both considered the discovery to be one of "great scientific interest." Dr. Pope, in a letter to the *Times* dated March 30, 1947, said:

This raises the further question whether it will not perhaps verify the Chinese tradition of their first (Hsia) dynasty, which it has been fashionable among Western sinologists to question. The next dynasty, the Shang, beginning about 1700 B.C., was long rejected by Western scholars also, until Chinese excavations at An-Yang established it beyond further doubt.

The Hsia Dynasty is now, I believe, accepted as real (the latest dates that I have for it are: "traditional" – 2205-1766 B.C., and "scientific" – 1994-1525 B.C.), but it is incredible to me that after the An-yang discoveries, there has ever been any doubt that something must have preceded the Shang (or Shang-Yin) Dynasty.

This latter is noted for its exquisite bronzes, which certainly were not developed overnight, and suggest a long period of sophisticated technological growth. In any case, Pope speculates that such a pyramid might be a Hsia royal tomb, and notes that it would be "one more demonstration of the Asia-wide importance of the cosmic mountain, and the astro-celestial cult of which it was a central feature."

Mr. Dobbins, using other references not specifically listed in his letter, says:

The Great Pyramid of Shensi is interesting – a virtual manmade mountain at 1000 feet high. This dwarfs the so-called "Great Pyramid" at Giza, which is about 470 feet high by 765 feet on the baseline. Despite the claims of "discovery" in 1947, the Georgia psychic and healer "Doc"

Anderson visited the thing prior to the war and testified to its size. He claimed that it was made of earth or clay, and had a leveled top on which perched the ruins of some kind of temple.

Apparently the locals wouldn't let him get a closer look. And, apparently, it is located near the "field" of smaller pyramids. This group covers an area of some ten square miles. There are possibly more pyramidal structures here than in all the rest of the world put together! And all are oriented along the north-south line, like the Egyptian examples. These Chinese pyramids have not been dated yet, and I wouldn't be too surprised if they are also the oldest findable.

This still leaves us with some problems. Issue #21 of *Doubt*, edited by Tiffany Thayer, contains the following article:

The story of Col. Maurice Sheahan was sent out by UPI, under a Shanghai date line, 3-28-47 old-style. Sheahan had seen, "several years ago," a pyramid in China bigger than any in Egypt. He had taken a photo from his plane. He had the photo at his home in Ontario, California, in San Bernardino County, near Los Angeles.

The next day, *The Los Angeles Daily News* printed a four-column photo, "First Picture of Great Chinese Pyramid." The photo credit was to "Acme Telephoto." Mr. Sheahan is not mentioned, neither is the picture dated, but if this is the photo taken by Sheahan "several years ago," why was it necessary to send it by wire from Ontario to Los Angeles? And since when does a village the size of Ontario have the facilities to send telexes?

Two days later, 3-31-47, AP sent its papers a story under a Nanking dateline, stating that "the provincial government had announced, following an investigation, that the reported discovery of a giant pyramid in Shensi province proved to be groundless."

This last move may have been "political," (i.e., a move designed to discourage foreign investigators, or simply to provide an excuse for saying "no" to anyone requesting permission to visit the area). On the other hand, the photograph shows one of the smaller pyramids, but contains nothing that makes it possible to determine its actual size or – let's be frank – its location.

Still, the photograph is itself a fact, and unless one wishes to call both Col. Sheahan and "Doc" Anderson liars, it is necessary to accept the photograph as evidence that there are enormous pyramids in China.

The largest artificial mound in Western Europe is Silbury Hill, near Avebury in England. It is only 130 feet high with a base covering more than five acres – small compared with the Great Pyramid, but still representing an enormous amount of labor (and because of its earthen construction, closer in spirit to the Shensi Pyramid. Its age and purpose are unknown; shafts dug into it at various times revealed no burials or chambers of any kind.

Enquiries sent to the Chinese on a number of subjects have so far gone unanswered, but we shall try again, to see whether they have changed their minds about the existence of these pyramids, and whether anything at all has been done about them.

MORE VIMANAS – JULY 1974

A subject that we have labored long to clear up is the business of the Vimanas, alleged to be flying machines operated by, or at least known to, the ancient inhabitants of the Indian subcontinent. A great many of the early books on ufology cited the Vimanas, as described in certain hoary Sanskrit texts, as proof of the existence of "saucers" in past ages.

The current wave of "ancient astronaut" books dealing specifically with the theme of extraterrestrial visitation in the distant past, and urging the thesis that these visitors established the main cultural traditions of our forebears, have not failed to include the Vimanas as a prominent feature of their argument.

Quite naturally, we wanted to know more about all of this. Unfortunately, we have been less than successful in our attempts to locate either definitive texts or complete translations of those fragments that mention the Vimanas. What little we have been able to establish, to date, has been intriguing, but seems not to interest Sanskrit scholars sufficiently to goad them into producing the kind of detailed examination that is clearly called for here.

In sum, it appears that there are, in fact, authentic ancient texts, of a quasi-religious nature, that describe flying machines and certain military applications for the craft. The motive power for the machines is said to derive from mercury. But whether these texts are really technical descriptions of craft observed at close range millennia ago, or merely striking examples of poetic and religious imagery, is a question still unanswered.

How it can be that a matter so fascinating as this fails to excite even a modicum of interest amongst those Sanskrit scholars who might be in a position to nail it all down, once and for all, is beyond us. The only consolation we can find in this sorry state of affairs is the thought that if specialists generally were to begin taking a good hard look at the bizarre and anomalous events in their fields, our SITU group would be out of business.

It seems that our journal, *Pursuit*, is read in India, and that our interest in Vimanas somehow came to the attention of an organization called the International Academy of Sanskrit Research in Mysore, India. The Institute was engaged in preparing a translation of a Sanskrit text dealing with Vimanas, and they sent us an advance brochure, which we published in Pursuit (Vol. 3, No. 4).

When the book arrived, we were pleased to note that the publisher mentioned the interest shown in the subject by SITU as one of the reasons that the book had been published. However, certain other comments in the Introduction rather puzzled us, as it seems that the volume is something other than the long-awaited definitive word on Vimanas that we had anticipated.

Mr. G. R. Josyer, Director of the Academy, explained the origin of the manuscript as follows: "There is no written material for the vast volume of Vedas, Upanishads, Shastras, and Puranas, which have come down for over 10,000 years as a patrimony, not only for India, but for mankind in general. They remain embedded in the ether of the sky, to be revealed – like television – to gifted mediums of occult perception."

Elsewhere, the author of the manuscripts is described as a man "gifted with occult perception," and his manuscript as a "revelation." The composition of the manuscript is described thusly: "On 1-18-1918, he began to dictate *Vymanika Sastra* to Mr. Venkatachala Sarma, who took down the whole in 23 exercise books up to 2-8-1923."

This book, then, is not a translation of an ancient Sanskrit text, but a manuscript produced between 1918 and 1923. It is apparently one of that class of clairvoyant productions known as "automatic writing."

In any event, the occult or psychic source of the book is clearly described and acknowledged by the editor and translator, and as such, it falls into one of those fields of knowledge that SITU eschews. We would not, however, dismiss this book merely on that point. It is the material lodged between the covers that is our primary concern.

In this regard, we can say that *Vymaanika-Shastra or Aeronautics by Maharashi Bharadwaaja, Propounded by the Venerable Subbaraya Sastry* (the official title of the book) strikes us as being fairly typical of the quality and usefulness of "revealed" literature in general. Rather than comment further on the specifics of the construction and operation of Vimanas, as revealed to and by the Venerable Mr. Sastry, we herewith reproduce a few passages from this elaborately bound volume:

> Next, the pratibimba-arka-kiranaakarshana naala, or tube for attracting the reflection of the solar rays...

> According to "Naalikaa-nirnaya," the essence of squash gourd, juice of momardica, 2 parts of the salt of the two-wheeled root vegetable, 3 parts of salt of simhamoola, 122nd type of glass, essence of white mica, jelly stone, borax, root of Bengal-madder, thorn at the root of bamboo, lead, mercury – these 15 ingredients are to be mixed in the proportion of 5, 12, 4, 3, 7, 3, 11,4,9, 12, 20, 18, 12, 5, 20.

> The mixture should be filled in the crucible known as *samayarglka*, and heated in the furnace of the same name, and heated to the degree of 315, with the aid of bellows called *suraghaa*. The resulting liquid should be poured into the mirrormaking machine. The resulting product will be a fine *bimbaarkakiranaadarsha*, or reflected solar ray-attracting mirror. This should be fixed in the central portion of the vimana, and in the 10th kendra, with five circled screws.

> Now we deal with the crest crystal of the vimana. The crest-crystals are of 103 kinds. They are named in "Mani-kalpa-pradeepika" as belonging to the 12th class of 32 groups of crystals. Their names are shankara, shaantaka, kharva, bhaaskara...

Ninety-nine more names followed. We have been asking ever since if there are any risk-takers out there, who would like to fire up the bellows and experiment with these unusual and amorphously measured ingredients, but so far – as we expected – no brave souls have come forward.

CHAPTER 3

In a book published in 1977, *Our Ancestors Came From Outer Space*, I disclosed my discovery of the Nineveh Constant of 2268 million days. This is now understood to be a constant of the universe, and an exact multiple of any astronomical cycle thus far known.

At the time of my discovery, I believed that the 2268 number was familiar only to, and used only by, Sumerian and Egyptian astronomers. That was a mistake, as an American scientist named Hugh Harleston made abundantly clear when his mathematical analysis of the ruins of Teotihuacán showed that the Grand Avenue in the once-dominant metropolis near Mexico City had a length of 2400 meters or 2268 ancient Mexican yards.

Since the dimensions, in yards, of all the city's buildings, and all the intervals between buildings, were exact fractions of 2268 yards, it became apparent that this number was as familiar to the ancient Mexicans as it was to the Egyptians (who used it to measure volume) and to the Sumerians (who used it to measure time). Awareness that the number 2268 had been an important measure of space and time gave encouragement to a search for the true origin of the number.

According to popular supposition, Teotihuacán was built by the Aztecs; actually, it could be much older. Until recently, it was almost impossible to measure exact dimensions of the city, or any of the ruined structures that lay within it. Investigations had been attempted without the prerequisite removal of encrusting soil and vegetation (which has been called "as strong as steel cable"). Subsequent restorations proceeded without anyone bothering to respect the original dimensions.

Adding to the confusion were those American books that identified the structures correctly, but gave only approximate dimensions in feet rounded to the nearest foot – enough of a difference to frustrate the efforts of those who sought to prove a precise relationship between the dimensions of the monuments and the spaces between them.

The research situation was somewhat improved when Swiss scientist Henri Stierlin published a remarkable study of the ruins, in which the dimensions were indicated in meters and centimeters on scaled drawings of the monuments. Thus, it became possible to obtain useful averages between the American dimensions in feet, and the Swiss dimensions in meters.

Further contributing to improved investigations of Mexican pyramids was a beautiful book published ten years ago by Peter Tompkins, which included a mathematical analysis of the dimensions by Hugh Harleston.

As might be expected in such a case, the dimensions given by Harleston were not exactly the same as those published by Stierlin. Both men found these ruins very difficult to measure, and each one did the work in a slightly different way. Even now, the monuments are not completely free of dirt and debris. The only sure way to obtain exact intervals and dimensions would be to use electronic distance-measuring equipment, targeting reflectors placed at the tops and corners of the monuments – exactly what I am planning to do as soon as possible.

Some of the discrepancies may also have percolated from Harleson's enthusiasm for crediting the architects of Teotihuacán with a knowledge of mathematics they simply did not have. Harleston assumed that all the monuments in the city had been built with a special yard representing the twelfth root of two meters, or 1.059463 meters.

Although I am willing to accept the likelihood that ancestral Mexicans knew as much about the metric system as many other ancient civilizations, I cannot believe that they could have extracted the twelfth root of two without access to a very good table of logarithms or the use of a better-than-rudimentary calculator.

It seems more likely that the builders of Teotihuacán designed the length of their Grand Avenue in such a way that it represented *both* 2400 meters and 2268 yards, thus establishing a yard of 1.0582 meters. If we use this value for the Mexican yard, we find almost exactly the same dimensions, whether indicated in meters by Stierlin, or indicated in feet by other scientists.

Small discrepancies notwithstanding, Harleston's measurements and calculations are extraordinary. He reconstructed, from the intervals and dimensions of these ruins, most of the mathematical formulas and astronomical cycles used by ancient civilizations – the Celts, the Egyptians, and the Sumerians in particular.

These discoveries make it difficult to believe that Teotihuacán was actually built by the Aztecs. Yet Harleston did not take into account a fundamental difference between our modern measuring system and the disparate method developed by the ancient Mexicans (and various other peoples of antiquity) for the measurement of length, area and volume.

Our system of measurement is based on the equivalence of the English yard and the French meter. Both are standards of linear measurement, and both are convertible to standards of area or surface measurement simply by "squaring." Our standard of volume measurement, the cube, is likewise a derivative of the linear standard; a cubic yard is a linear yard, and a cubic meter is a linear meter.

But many ancient people based their volume measurements on standards that were not merely three-dimensional extensions of their linear standards, but were more spontaneously derived from a countable quantity of things, or the size of a familiar container.

For example, the Egyptians were using, to measure length, a cubit of 0.525 meter; its cube was 0.144,703 cubic meters, and thus not very practical. In the construction of the Great Pyramid, however, they used a cubit of 0.524,148 meter; its cube was 0.144,000 meters, representing 144 kilograms of water or 16,000 kedets of 9 grams each – which shows that these ancients knew about the metric system or something very similar to it. This cubit corresponded to a yard of 1.048,296 meters and to a cubic yard of 1.152 cubic meters.

In the same manner, the Mexicans used, to measure length, a yard of 1.0582 meters, whose cube was an impractical 1.184,962, so they preferred to measure volume with a yard of 1.045,516 meters, whose cube was 1.142,857, exactly 8/7 of a cubic meter. In other words, the two volume-measuring units of the Egyptians and Mexicans were both exact fractions of a cubic meter, with the Egyptian cubit representing 126 thousandths of a Mexican cubic yard. This was an important discovery!

The number 126 is both a sacred Hebraic number (found everywhere in the Cabala) and a magic nuclear number – the last one of the series 2, 8, 20, 50, 82, and 126, representing the numbers of neutrons and protons that are necessary for the stability of the nucleus. The number 126 can thus be considered both the symbol of nuclear stability and the homologue of 280, which is the highest known quantic number. It is also the symbol of energy in the equivalence between mass and energy.

Of course, one may wonder what could have been the nuclear knowledge of the ancient pyramid builders, but without going that far afield, we cannot help noticing that if we multiply by 126 the volume of the Great Pyramid (18 million cubic cubits), we obtain 2268 million cubic cubits.

Moreover, if we measure the volume of that pyramid in Mexican cubic yards, it comes to a total of 2268 million cubic yards. The numbers 126 and 2268 have played a very important part in the mathematical calculations of our ancestors all over the world.

Such evidence acknowledges the common origin of various ancient civilizations whose vestiges have been discovered on both sides of the

Atlantic Ocean – the probable place of common origin, namely Atlantis, having disappeared into that ocean twelve thousand years ago.

Such research led me to discover that the volumes of all known pyramids are proportional to each other; also, that they are exact fractions of the volume of the earth (which our ancestors seem to have estimated in billions of billions). If we divide with thirteen zeros the volume of the earth by the numbers 35, 42, 48, 105 and 288, for example, we successively obtain the volume of the pyramids of Cholula in Mexico, Cheops and Chephren in Egypt, Teotihuacán in Mexico, and Poverty Point in Louisiana.

It then becomes obvious that all of these numbers and therefore all of these volumes, are proportional to each other *and* to the volume of the earth; and they are also related to the Constant of Nineveh of 2268 million days.

Recently, I also found that the base areas of many pyramids were exact multiples of 36, 49, 64, 81 or 121 square meters, and therefore were exact fractions of the surface of the earth, as it might have been estimated by our ancestors: 510,984,936 square kilometers, or about 197,292,400 square miles. This would explain why pyramids have base sides of 231, 216, 189, 108 or 84 meters, for example.

Ever since I discovered the Nineveh Constant ten years ago, I have felt sure that this unit of time must have its equivalent in space, in the form of a unit of length, surface, volume, perhaps also energy. For we have known since Einstein that energy is a function of both time and space.

For energy, I have found in the nuclear series the numbers 18 and 126, whose product is equal to 2268, and the number 36,288, which is 16 times 2268. For length, the granite coffer in the King's Chamber of the Great Pyramid has a length of 2268 millimeters, and the Grand Avenue in Teotihuacán has a length of 2268 Mexican yards. For surface, I have found that both the base of the Mayan pyramid of Copan and the first platform of the Sumerian ziggurat of Ur have areas of 2268 square meters, which, of course, belies coincidence.

It is among the volumes that I have found the largest number of correspondences. The Pyramid of Chephren had an original volume of 2268 thousand cubic meters, equivalent to 7/8 of the volume of the Cheops pyramid, which had a volume of 2268 thousand Mexican cubic yards. This is what led me to compute the volumes of all the pyramids and thus discover that they were all proportional to each other, and exact multiples of a basic volume of 96 cubic meters.

Knowing the original dimensions of the Pyramid of Cheops in Egypt and the Pyramid of the Sun in Teotihuacán allowed me to make a fantastic discovery, which certainly will never be accepted by academic or "official" scientists.

Ten years ago, while I was computing the original dimensions of the Pyramid of Cheops, I noticed that its faces were slightly concave, with the middle line or apothem clearly visible. I postulated that the continuation of this line on the northern face beyond the apex should make it possible to find the point of intersection of the line with the celestial equator, and to calculate the altitude of that point above the surface of the Earth or the distance from its center. I felt that such figures might very well have been significant for the ancient Egyptians, too.

I further noted that an artificial satellite of the Earth placed at that distance (21,000 kilometers from its surface or 27,400 kilometers from its center) would have a revolution period of 12.3115 hours, exactly one half of the rotation period of Mars, which is 24.6230 hours. In other words, a projection of the apothem on the north face of the Great Pyramid intersects the celestial equator at a point where an artificial Earth satellite would make two revolutions around the earth, while Mars would make one rotation around its axis.

Such a satellite would always see the same face of Mars on every other turn, and the opposite face on intermediate turns. Two stations on Mars would thus be sufficient to maintain contact with the satellite every twelve hours, and four stations on the Earth would be enough to keep a permanent contact between the satellite and the Earth.

We shall probably never know if those who built the Great Pyramids, whether they were gods or men, had the means to install bases on Mars, or knew enough to position Earth satellites to maintain permanent contact with the bases. But I was nonetheless proud of myself for having envisioned such a fantastic possibility.

How wrong I was! What I had missed turned out to be even more extraordinary than what I had sensed.

In April 1976, 1 received from London a letter written by a British gentleman named Saunders. He had read about my research work on the Great Pyramid when my book was published in French. He thought I might be interested in a discovery that he had made. Believe it or not, he, too, had found the connection between the apothem of the Great Pyramid and a possible Mars-synchronous artificial satellite of the earth.

And he had found much more. He had discovered that if one traces a line through the earth between the center of the base of the Great Pyramid, which is located at 29.9790 North – 31.1330 East, and the center of the base of the Pyramid of the Sun in Teotihuacán, which is located at 19.6940 North – 98.8440 West, the continuation of the line would intersect the celestial equator at the same distance from the center of the Earth as that of the Mars-synchronous satellite.

There were a few differences, of course. I had found for the satellite an altitude of 20,777 kilometers, while Saunders had found 21,229 kilometers in the first case, and 20,884 in the second. He had made his calculations with the famous astronomer Duncan Lunan, and Saunders is probably the one who is right.

We had used different data and different calculation techniques; the coincidence was therefore all the more remarkable. However, since Saunders did not get the same result in both cases, some doubt about his accuracy will likely remain.

Either our data and calculation techniques are incorrect and we should find, for example, 21,330 kilometers, which is the circumference of Mars; or, we are dealing with a fantastic coincidence, where the builders of the two pyramids never thought of establishing bases on Mars or launching artificial satellites to maintain permanent contact.

Saunders was an indefatigable researcher. By studying the possible relationships between the two pyramids and the earth, and Mars and its two satellites, Phobos and Deimos, he discovered twelve distinct "coincidences" that are difficult to believe, even for one who, like myself, has already encountered many strange situations for which coincidence is the only reasonable explanation.

Saunders first found that the mass of the Great Pyramid, which is about six million tons when multiplied by a million billions, is equal to the mass of the earth (six thousand billions of billions of tons). Then, the distance from Mars to the Sun (228 million kilometers) represents about a billion times the base side of that pyramid (230 meters). The eccentricity of the orbit of Mars is about equal to that of the axis of the King's Chamber of the Great Pyramid, and the apothem of the north face intersects the celestial equator at an altitude about equal to the circumference of Mars (21,330 kilometers).

Some of the entries on Saunders' list merely note the obvious. For example, the largest volcano on Earth, in Hawaii, is located at a latitude of about 19 degrees; the largest volcano on Mars, called Nix Olympica, and the Pyramid of the Sun in Mexico, are also located at latitudes of about 19 degrees.

Other relationships, though less apparent, may be more significant, to wit: The number of revolutions of Deimos during a rotation of the earth is equal to 11/14, which is the ratio between the half-base and the height of the Great Pyramid. The number of revolutions of Phobos during a rotation of the earth is equal to 22/7, which is the ancient pi factor, and the ratio between the half-perimeter and the height of the pyramid. These relationships suggest that the locations of the satellites may have been artificially predetermined.

If we juxtapose the Moon and the Earth, the triangle formed by lines drawn from the center of the Moon and to the two opposite ends of the diameter of the earth, is similar to a cross-section of the Great Pyramid in Egypt. If we were to build a "Great Pyramid" on the Moon at the same latitude as on the Earth, the continuation of the pyramid's apothem would intersect the equatorial plane of the Moon at the same altitude as that of Phobos above the surface of Mars.

The height of Deimos, above Mars, is equal to 22/7 of the radius of the earth. If we trace from Deimos a line passing through a latitude of 19 degrees on Mars, that line emerges on the other side at a latitude of 25-1/4 degrees, and if we build a "Great Pyramid" at that point, the continuation of its apothem will intersect the celestial equator of Mars at the altitude of Phobos.

So far, this is the last of Saunders' twelve coincidences. They could be nothing more, or a lot more, than an extraordinary array of coincidences without correlation. I digress here, to encourage anyone who is sufficiently interested, to rework the calculations and decide for himself or herself what cosmic program, if any, could have been deliberately planned by our ancestors, and for what purpose. Meanwhile, I shall leave to friend Saunders the credit and the responsibility for his discoveries, for I am convinced he has found a goldmine of cosmic information.

In general, I do not believe in miracles. I do not expect professional astronomers to take these discoveries seriously, but maybe one of them will someday have the curiosity to check them out and find the courage to publish the results of his calculations. Perhaps that still would not prove that our ancestors were visited by astronauts from Mars several thousand years ago.

But at least, it would give us some very good reasons to believe that we are not alone in the universe. Meanwhile, we should try to learn everything we can about ancient Mexican astronomy and the astronomical computer of Teotihuacán in particular. The archeological complex of Teotihuacán was an important center of religious observance, but it was also a remarkable astronomical observatory and a fantastic cosmic computer.

Recent discoveries show that every dimension of the sacred city had an astronomical or mathematical meaning; and several of these dimensions were so interrelated as to replicate some of the constants of nuclear physics used by contemporary scientists.

It now seems almost certain that the architects of Teotihuacán were using, as a unit of length, a yard of 1.0582 meters, which was an exact fraction of that modern unit derived from the circumference of the earth. They had a mile of 1600 meters or 1512 yards, a stadium of 200 meters or 189 yards, and smaller units of 54, 27, 18, and 9 yards, whose names have been lost.

All of these numbers are exact fractions of the sacred number 2268, a number which has been found in the ruins of several ancient civilizations and seems to have been a basic unit of time and space around the world several thousand years ago.

Thus, the measuring system of the Mexicans was based on the number 9, while that of the Egyptians was based on 10, that of the Chaldeans on 12, that of the Mayas on 20, and that of the Sumerians on 60. Obviously, Teotihuacán was not built by the Mayas. Moreover, the number 2268 is also found in the Nineveh Constant of the Sumerians, which indicates that the Mexican and Sumerian civilizations were related or shared a common origin.

The original dimensions of the Teotihuacán religious center are best described in Mexican yards as follows: The total length between the southern facade of the northern buildings and the southern end of the platform of the Citadel is exactly 2268 yards.

That length can be divided into four parts: 1) The distance between the northern buildings and the axis of the Pyramid of the Moon – 207 yards; 2) the distance between the axis of that pyramid and that of the Pyramid of the Sun – 720 yards; 3) the distance between the axis of that pyramid and that of the Pyramid of Quetzalcoatl – 1134 yards; and 4) the distance between the axis of that pyramid and the southern end of the platform of the Citadel – 207 yards (as at the other end of the city).

The oblique distance between the center of the Pyramid of the Moon and that of the Pyramid of the Sun is 756 yards, which represents one third of the total length and twice the Saturn synodic cycle of 378 days.

Another interesting distance is that between the axis of the Grand Avenue and the center of the Pyramid of Quetzalcoatl, which is 288 yards – the sacred number of Tiahuanaco and the Cabala, as well as a magic nuclear number that has been found all over the world and represents two cycles of conjunction of Mercury and Venus.

The three principal pyramids of Teotihuacán were built with a special yard of 1.0455 meters, the cube of which is equal to 8/7 of a cubic meter; their volumes are always multiples of eight cubic meters or seven Mexican cubic yards. The ingenious technique is comparable to that of the Egyptians; they built the Pyramid of Cheops with a special cubit having a cube equal to 0.144 or 18/125 of a cubic meter.

The original dimensions of the Pyramid of the Sun were 216 x 216 x 63 yards. Its original volume was 907,200 cubic yards, or 1,036,800 milliliters. The dimensions are in agreement with Harleston's and the volume with that of Stierlin. The volume is equal to one third of the volume of the Pyramid of Cholula, and to 40 percent of the volume of Cheops.

The present dimensions of the Pyramid of the Moon are 144 x 128 x 42 yards, which corresponds to a volume of 241,920 cubic yards, or 276,490 milliliters. However, the Pyramid of the Moon has been restored several times for purposes of foreign policy or domestic political propaganda. (The politicians probably demanded speedy completion of these restorations, so large quantities of material were removed and used elsewhere without anyone protesting, or perhaps even noticing, that the dimensions had been changed.)

Comparisons with other monuments at Teotihuacán make clear what happened to the Pyramid of the Moon. Only the latter is rectangular; and the width of 128 yards is the one and only dimension in the whole complex that is not divisible by 9.

It therefore seems likely that the Pyramid of the Moon was originally square, and that its dimensions were 144 x 144 x 42 yards, with an original volume of 268,800 cubic yards, or 307,200 cubic meters, which would have been 3.375 times smaller than the volume of the Pyramid of the Sun. Since the volume of a cubic foot is also 3.375 times smaller than a cubic cubit, the volume of the Pyramid of the Moon in cubic feet would have been the same as that of the Pyramid of the Sun in cubic cubits. The equivalence gives support to my assumption.

The original dimensions of the Pyramid of Quetzalcoatl were 63 x 63 x 21 yards, corresponding to a volume of 22,680 cubic yards, or 25,920 cubic meters. This volume is very interesting; 2268 is related to the Nineveh Constant, while 2592 is related to the Pyramid of Cheops and to the precession of the equinoxes.

This seems to indicate a common origin for the Mexican, Egyptian, and Sumerian civilizations, or at least, frequent cultural connections across the oceans. The volume also represents 270 unit volumes of 96 cubic meters, which is the volume of the Pyramid of the Sun divided by 40, or that of the earth divided by 42 with 15 zeros. It also represents one-hundredth the volume of the Great Pyramid.

Before the investigations of Stierlin and Harleston, the first serious research work at the ruins of Teotihuacán was done by a young American scientist of French origin named René Millon. He arrived in Mexico City in 1950, after he had completed his anthropology courses at Columbia University in New York.

Following a few years of fieldwork, he obtained for Columbia a grant from the National Science Foundation, in 1962, to fund the production of an exact map of the ruins by means of aerial photography. A constant altitude of 1200 meters would be maintained, and grids established to limits of 500 meters on each side of the centerline of the Grand Avenue.

The camera work aloft consumed the least amount of time allotted to the project. Assembling the photographs and taking ground measurements of everything recorded on the films required five years of hard work. When the finished map was placed on public view in 1967, it revealed with startling clarity the Teotihuacán of more than two thousand years ago: a true metropolis, adequate for a population of 200,000.

Wide avenues, many pyramids of different sizes, and more than 2600 residential buildings covered an area of twenty-five square kilometers, or more than 6,000 acres. Furthermore, it had to have been built according to a rectangular plan prepared in advance of construction.

The oldest part of the city, where the three principal pyramids are located in an area of about six square kilometers or 1500 acres, is more than four thousand years old; some archaeologists believe that it may antedate the eruption of the Xitli volcano about eight thousand years ago.

Teotihuacán could very well be the oldest city in North America, just as Tiahuanaco could be the oldest city in South America. Even between the two names there is a curious possible linkage. Both names could have sprung from common roots: "theos, " the Greek word for divinity, and "huaco," which means death or grave in various local dialects. Both names allow only one translation: "City of the Dead Gods."

René Millon seems to have been the first to think that Teotihuacán – like Stonehenge, the Great Pyramid, and the Tower of Babel – could have been designed and used primarily, or adjunctively, as astronomical observatories to explore the mysterious relationships of mankind, space, and time.

He was also the first to notice that the dimensions of most monuments and intervals at Teotihuacán were always fractions or multiples of a standard length of 57 meters, and that seven times that length represented exactly four hundred meters.

We now know that Millon was right. Four hundred meters represent 378 yards, and 57.143 meters represent 54 yards or six times nine yards. There is no doubt, then, that our evaluation of the Mexican yard is correct, and that it takes 37.8 million yards to measure the circumference of the earth, or 360 million yards to measure the distance to the Moon.

Harleston does not quite agree with that value, but I still have a great admiration for him; he was the first to discover that the sacred number 2268, which had been used by the Sumerians to measure time, had also been used by the Mexicans to measure space.

This is a significant archaeological discovery, for it shows that these civilizations had a common origin, and that they had begun to probe the wondrous relationships between time and space thousands of years ago.

The Pyramid of the Sun was built in such a way that, on the lower part of the fourth step, only the north and west sides were in the shade at noon on March 21 and September 21, the respective days of the spring and autumn equinoxes.

This phenomenon, which lasted only sixty seconds, allowed the ancient Mexican astronomers to determine the exact time on those dates when the Sun crossed the celestial equator, thus setting the start and the midpoint of their astronomical year.

In no way could this be any kind of coincidence; complicated calculations, very accurate measurements and perfect site-orientation are necessary to obtain the "shade effect" at the precise times of the equinoxes.

Another number of importance to the ancient Mexican calendar-makers was 52, found several times between the small temples located on the outer edge of the Citadel; the apparent reference was to 52 years or 65 heliacal risings of Venus. And around the court of the Citadel, measurements of 365 yards are found three times, and 366 yards once – which probably represented a year of 365-1/4 days, very close to the length of our tropical year.

Harleston made a fantastic discovery that might be the major achievement of his research in Teotihuacán. One day, when he had started from the east-west axis of the Citadel and was going north on the Grand Avenue, he discovered some stone markers at distances of 36, 72, 96, 144, 288, 520 and 945 yards.

He found the distances proportional to the distances from the Sun of the first seven planets, including Ceres, which seems to be a remnant of Phaeton, the planet that orbited between Jupiter and Saturn until a few million years ago (when it exploded). Harleston reasoned that the Grand Avenue had been designed as a reproduction of our entire solar system!

CHAPTER 4

Renowned author Erich von Däniken contends that our present pencil-shaped rockets are impractical, even dangerous! What follows is a case for the sphere as the perfect shape for intergalactic travel, supported by historical evidence.

THE SPHERE: THE IDEAL SHAPE FOR SPACECRAFT – ERICH VON DÄNIKEN – 1978

All of the rockets in service today are pencil-shaped. Is this absolutely necessary? Surely there is constant proof that the pencil shape is neither necessary nor ideal in airless space. Anyone watching those odd-shaped lunar modules and boosters trying to navigate can sense that there must be a better way.

The liberation of higher propulsive energy is the key that would lead to the manufacture of new types of spacecraft. The time when technology will have incredible energies at its disposal is no longer so far away. When that time comes, it could lead to pure photon propulsion units that can reach a velocity close to the speed of light, and can provide propulsion for an almost unlimited period.

Soon we shall no longer have to economize on every pound of payload, as we do today – when every pound that a spacecraft takes on a journey to the moon is needed. Once the fuel problem is solved, spacecraft can be built in a very different shape.

Old texts and archaeological finds around the world have convinced me that the first spacecraft that reached the earth, many thousands of years ago, were spherical. And I am sure that the spacecraft of the future will, once again, be spherical.

I am no rocket designer, but there are a couple of reflections that we can make and which seem completely convincing. A sphere has no forward or aft, no above or below, no right or left. It offers the same surface in every position and directional, making it the ideal shape for the cosmos, which also has no above or below, forward or aft.

Let us take a walk around a space sphere that still seems like a science-fiction dream today. But let's not skimp matters. Imagine a sphere with a diameter of 17,000 feet. This monster stands on springy, retractable spider legs. Like an ocean liner, the interior is divided into decks of various sizes.

Around the belly of the gigantic ball, at its equator, runs a massive ring housing the twenty or more propulsion units that can be swiveled through 180 degrees – a relatively simple technical feat. When the countdown has reached zero, they will radiate concentrated light waves, amplified a million-fold.

If the cosmic sphere is to rise from the surface of the planet or one of the launching areas stationed in orbit, the propulsion units shoot their columns of light directly down onto the launching pad, giving the sphere a tremendous thrust.

Once the sphere has reached the extra-gravitational field and is on its course to a fixed star, the propulsion units around its equator will only be fired, now and then, for course corrections. There is no risk of the sphere moving out of its flight path in a way that might endanger the crew, because it can immediately adapt itself to any situation.

Besides, something happens that will be very pleasant for the astronauts. The sphere begins to rotate of its own accord. In this way, an artificial gravity is created in all the external rooms that decreases the state of weightlessness so much that conditions are almost the same as on Earth.

It is important to realize that this kind of space-sphere course correction, in any direction, is possible without danger. The propulsion units mounted on the steel girdle permit quick turns in any direction. Billiards players will easily catch on to the idea. If a right turn is needed, the sphere gets a light touch from a steering jet mounted on the left, and vice versa.

Spherical spacecraft of this kind may have traversed the galaxies millennia ago. Shooting close to the speed of light, our modern astronauts will only sense the tempo as a slow, soft floating away. Time will seem to stand still in their craft.

I won't expand on these excursions to utopia. Science-fiction writers have described imaginary spaceships of the future already. My sphere story is solely intended to prepare the reader's imagination for a perfectly serious idea. Suppose we examine the first legends of mankind's creation with this sphere in mind.

The Popol Vuh contains a wonderful account. This secret book, called one of the "great writings of the dawn of mankind," was the only scripture of the Quiché Indians, or Mayans, around Lake Atitlan in the Central American country of Guatemala.

Its comprehensive creation myth claims that men only partially stem from this earth. The "gods" created the "first beings endowed with reason," but destroyed all of the unsuccessful examples. After performing their earthly tasks, the gods rose into Heaven again, to the place where the "heaven's heart" is, namely to Dabavil, to him "who sees in the darkness."

Is this the reason the Quiché Indians were imbued with the concept of gods who dwelt in stone spheres, and who could emerge from the stone? Does the ballgame cult of this tribe, of which *The Popol Vuh* tells, have its roots in this creation myth? Is the ballgame a cosmic and magical rite, a symbol of the gods' flight to the stars?

Among the creation stories that strengthen my theory, the myth of Chibcha (i.e., mankind) is a real jewel. The historical home of these people, whom the Spaniards discovered in 1538, is on the east plateau of Colombia.

The Spanish chronicler Pedro Simon describes the myth of the Chibcha in his *Noticias Historiales de Las Conquistas de Tierra Firme en Las Indias Occidentales*:

> It was night. There was still something of the world. The light was closed up in a big "something house," and came out of it. This "something house" is "Chiminigagua," and it hid the light in it, so that it came out. In the brightness of the light, things began to come into being.

I can see that it must have been difficult for translators and interpreters to find a clear-cut equivalent for the word "something house." But how lucky for us that they left this concept and did not replace it by a fanciful synonym. Otherwise, we might not be able to interpret correctly the significance of this tradition and grasp its full importance.

But now we can measure the "something house" against our present knowledge. As the Chibcha had never seen a spacecraft before, they obviously did not know what to call it. So they paraphrased it in words that were familiar to them: Something like a house had landed, and the "gods" had come out of it.

The traditions of the Incas in Peru say that even before the world was created, a man named Uiracocha existed (i.e., Viracocha, later called Quetzalcoatl), whose full name Uiracocha Tachayachachic means "creator of the world things." This god had originally been *both* man and woman. He/she settled in Tiahuanaco, and created a race of giants there.

Is there perhaps a direct relation between the monolith in Tiahuanaco, the magnificent Gate of the Sun, and the traditional story of the creation? Are we too arbitrarily interpreting, say, the saga of the "golden egg," which came from the cosmos and whose passengers began the creation of men? If we take it at its face value, is it not an authentic account of a spacecraft from unknown stars?

This golden or gleaming egg that fell from heaven is a veritable *leitmotif* in mankind's traditional stories of creation. On Easter Island, the gods were worshipped as lords of space. Among them, Makemake is the god of the dwellers in the air. His symbol is the egg!

There are two strange books in Tibet called *Kantyua* and *Tantyua*. The *Kantyua* alone comprises 108 parchment volumes, which number 1,083 books in nine large divisions. "Kantyua" means "the translated word of Buddha," and the sacred texts of Lamaism are collected in it. *Kantyua* has the same kind of importance as the *Koran* has for Islam.

"Tantyua" means "the translated doctrine," and is a 225-volume commentary on *Kantyua*. These Chinese printed books take up so much room that they are preserved in the cellars of several villages that lie hidden in the mountain valleys of Tibet.

The separate parts of the texts are carved on wooden blocks 3 feet long, 4 to 8 inches thick, and 6 inches wide. Since no more than eight blocks can go on one parchment page, it is understandable that the volumes have to be housed in the cellars of whole villages. Only one percent of these texts, whose original date is not fixed, have been translated.

In both of these mysterious works, there is constant mention of "pearls in the sky" and transparent spheres, in which the gods dwell, that show themselves to men at great intervals. If there were purposeful and coordinated research on *Kantyua* and *Tantyua*, we would probably learn a very great deal about the "gods" and their former activities on Earth.

In the Indian world, the *Rig Veda* is considered to be the oldest book. The "Song of Creation" that it tells nicely describes that state of weightlessness and soundlessness that reigns in the infinity of the universe. I quote from Paul Frischauer's book, *It Is Written*:

> In those days, there was neither not-being nor being. Neither the atmosphere nor the sky was above. What flew to [and fro] and from where? In whose keeping? What was the unfathomable? In those times, there was neither death nor immortality. There was not a sign of day and night.
>
> This one breathed according to its own law, without currents of air. Everything else but this was not present. In the beginning, darkness was hidden in darkness. The life-powerful that was enclosed by the void, the one, was born by the might of its hot urgency.

We should take special notice of the phrase "the life powerful that was enclosed by the void." As twentieth-century people, we can hardly recognize this "Song of Creation" as anything but an account of a space journey. But who can explain convincingly why ancient peoples all over the world, who did not know of each other's existence, told stories of the creation with the same basic core?

In the old Chinese classic, *The Tao de Ching*, there is one of the most beautiful definitions of the origin of the cosmos, life, and Earth: "The meaning that one can invent is not the eternal meaning. The name that one can name is not the eternal name. Beyond the nameable lies the beginning of the world. On this side of the nameable lies the birth of creatures."

According to this definition, too, the "beginning of the world" lies outside our sphere; on this side, "this side of the nameable," lies only the "birth of creatures."

Egyptian priests provided the mummified dead with texts containing instructions for their future behavior on the other side. These books of the dead were very detailed; they contained advice covering every conceivable situation. The directives were meant to lead to reunion with the god Ptah.

One of the oldest prayers in these Egyptian books of the dead reads: "O' world-egg, hear me. I am Horus of millions of years. I am lord and master of the throne. Freed from evil, I traverse the ages and spaces that are endless."

I am always delighted when I can prove textual interpretations with pictures or, better still, tangible works by stonemasons. And circles, spheres, and balls can be found in abundance.

In the Tassili Mountains in the Algerian Sahara, figures in strange suits can be seen painted in hundreds of places on the rock faces. They wear round helmets with antennae on their heads, and seem to be floating weightlessly in space.

I should make special mention of the Tassili sphere, which the Frenchman Henri Lhote discovered on the underside of a semicircular rock. In a group of floating couples – a woman is pulling a man behind her – a sphere with four concentric circles is clearly visible.

On the upper edge of the sphere, a hatch is open and from it, a thoroughly modern-looking TV aerial protrudes. From the right half of the sphere stretches two unmistakable hands with outspread fingers. Five floating figures accompanying the sphere wear tight-fitting helmets on their heads, with white and red dots. Are they astronauts' helmets?

Circles and spheres, apparently strategically distributed, are found in countless places throughout the world. All spheres and circles – whether in creation myths, prehistoric drawings, or later reliefs and paintings – represent "god" or the "godhead." The rays are generally directed earthward. In my opinion, this universal custom gives us something to think about.

I am convinced that the traditional spheres and divine eggs have more than a mere religious and symbolic significance. The time has come to look at these signs from another point of view. The patterns of thought we have followed so far may be absolutely wrong. So far we have lacked the prerequisites to grasp fully the legacy of the "gods" contained in the monuments and documents of our primitive ancestors.

Spheres surrounded by rays, eggs, and flying spheres are not only found on cave walls and cliffs, ancient stone reliefs and cylinder seals, but also "in the round," made of hard stone, in many different parts of the world (generally scattered indiscriminately and in inhospitable country). In the United States, for example, stone balls have been found in Tennessee, Arizona, California, and Ohio.

In 1940, Professor Marcel Homet, the archaeologist now living in Stuttgart and author of the well-known book *Sons of the Sun*, discovered a gigantic stone egg, 328 feet long and 98 feet high, on the upper Rio Branco in North Amazonas, Brazil. On this colossal block, which was called Piedra Pintada, or "painted stone," Homet found countless letters, crosses, and sun symbols over a surface area of some 700 square yards. He assured me that there was not the slightest doubt that this magnificent specimen was no freak of nature, but stonemason's work carried out by countless hands over many decades.

But the real archaeological sensation in the ball catalog is in the small Central American state of Costa Rica. There, hundreds, if not thousands, of artificial stone balls lie about in the middle of the jungle and on high mountains, in river deltas and on hilltops. Their diameters vary between a few inches and eight feet. The heaviest balls excavated to date weigh several tons.

I had heard about this sensation, and because of it, I spent ten days in Costa Rica, a typical developing country that has so far been shunned by the vast mass of tourists. My journey turned out to be anything but a pleasure trip, but all the hardships were richly rewarded by what I saw.

The first balls I came across were lying around in flat country for no apparent reason. Then I found several groups of balls on the tops of hills. Some always lay in the center of the hill's longitudinal axis. I waded through the mud of a riverbed and found great groups of balls in strange formations that were unintelligible, although they must have been deliberate.

Forty-five balls have been lying in the burning sun of the white-hot Diquis Plain since time immemorial. Have they something to say that we are incapable of understanding? In order to satisfy my curiosity to see and photograph the balls near Piedras Blancas, southeast of the River Coto, we had to spend a whole day in a Land Rover to cover a distance of only sixty miles.

Time and again, we had to remove obstacles from the track, pull the Land Rover out of ruts, and grind around innumerable bends. Finally our vehicle would take us no farther. Our guide ran ahead of us, for an hour, and cleared the way of creatures. Without his precautions, we twice would have run into spider webs, of a size you simply cannot imagine. The poisonous bite of these loathsome creatures can be fatal.

At last, we stood before two enormous balls, both taller than we were, in the midst of the virgin forest. It is precisely because the stones near Piedras Blancas lay deep in the jungle that I had wanted to see them with my own eyes. It is said that these balls are only a few hundred years old. No one who has stood there, as I have, could believe that. The jungle itself is primeval. I am convinced that the balls must have lain there before the luxuriant vegetation began to thrive.

We may have managed to transplant the Egyptian site, Abu Simbel, to another site using all kinds of modern machinery, but I doubt whether we could deposit balls like these in a primeval forest.

I saw still more balls in Costa Rica. Fifteen giant balls lie in a dead straight line in Golfo Dulce. Four balls have been excavated from the muddy bed of the River Esquina. There are two balls on Camaronal Island, and several balls on the summit of the Cordillera Brunquera, in the neighborhood of the River Diquis.

Most of these mysterious balls are made of granite or lava. There is little chance, nowadays, of finding out the exact number of stone balls that once existed. Today, many fine specimens decorate gardens, parks, and public buildings. Since one ancient saga also related that gold could be found in the middle of the balls, many of them have been hacked to bits with hammer and chisel.

A strange thing is that there are no quarries for producing the balls anywhere near the sites where they have been found. Any trace that could lead us back to the manufacturers is missing.

During the clearing of woods and swamps at the foot of the Cordillera

Brunquera in 1940 and 1941, the archaeologist Doris Z. Stone discovered several artificial stones. She wrote a detailed account of them that closes with the resigned remark: "The balls of Costa Rica must be numbered among the unsolved megalithic puzzles of the world."

In fact, we do not know who made the stone balls; we do not know what tools were used for the work; we do not know for what purpose the balls were cut out of the granite; and we do not know when they were made. Everything that archaeologists say today about these "sky balls," as the natives call them, is pure speculation.

A local legend says that each ball represents the sun – an acceptable interpretation. But the archaeologists reject this version, because in these latitudes, the sun has always been represented as a golden orb, wheel, or disk, and never as a ball (even among the Incas, Mayas, and Aztecs).

One thing is quite certain. The stone balls cannot have originated without mechanical help. They are perfectly executed – absolutely spherical, with smoothly polished surfaces. Archaeologists who have investigated the balls of Costa Rica confirm that none of them deviates, in the slightest, from a given diameter. This precision implies that the men who made them had a good knowledge of geometry and possessed the appropriate technical implements.

If the stonemasons had first buried the raw material in the earth and then worked on the protruding section, unevenness and inaccuracies would inevitably have resulted because the distances to the part stuck in the ground could no longer have been checked. This primitive procedure is out of the question.

The raw material must have been transported from somewhere, because there are no nearby quarries, and that alone must have been very arduous. There are considerable obstacles to transporting material in this region. I have noticed that whenever archaeologists cannot explain gigantic feats of transport, they have recourse to the so-called rolling theory. But this is pitifully inadequate, when one sees the giant balls on the tops of mountains. (One expert told me that at least 24 tons of raw material is needed to make a stone ball weighing 16 tons.)

Having seen the miraculous stone balls, I asked the Costa Ricans about their origin and meaning, but was met with silence and suspicion. The natives remain superstitious in their heart of hearts. Two archaeologists I questioned in the Museo Nacional of San José explained that the creation of the balls was connected with a religious cult that worshipped stars using magic symbols.

I could not solve the mystery of the stone balls, but my suspicion has increased. The prehistoric balls may be directly linked with the visitations of unknown intelligences, who landed on our planet in a ball. They already knew that the sphere is the most suitable shape for interstellar space flights.

CHAPTER 5

John T. Omohundro is an assistant professor of anthropology at the State University of New York at Potsdam.

VON DÄNIKEN'S CHARIOTS: A PRIMER IN THE ART OF COOKED SCIENCE – JOHN T. OMOHUNDRO – 1976

In 1974, *Playboy* asked Erich Von Däniken, "Are you the most brilliant satirist in German literature of the last century?" He answered, "The answer is yes and no. In some part, I mean what I say seriously. In other ways, I mean to make people laugh… I am not a scientific man, and if I had written a scientific book, it would have been calm and sober, and nobody would talk about it."

Were it not for the fact that Erich von Däniken has millions of otherwise intelligent people discussing his book and theories seriously, I would prefer to write a parody of his style. But I fear his readership might believe me, too.

I ignored his books for four years, but now I cannot teach my students or talk to my academic colleagues without his name souring my day. It is out of his hands, now, this chariot thing. It has reached the people, and for reasons that are their own, they have made von Däniken a prophet, and me, a defender of the Establishment. Why is this book so popular? Von Däniken, it seems, has written one of the scriptures of a new cult.

What he says, people obviously want to hear. Throughout history, cultures subjected to stressful situations have responded with cataclysmic religious reformations, often as a substitute for, or supplement to, political rebellion; the Zulu Uprising in Africa, the Sepoy Rebellion in India, the New Guinea Cargo Cults, the Ghost Dance of the Plains Indians, the Taiping Rebellion in China, and the Luddites and Anabaptists in Europe are some of the famous examples.

Anthropologists call them revitalization movements, messianic cults, and so forth, and take them quite seriously. Though they vary greatly, they have certain characteristics in common: a humorless fanaticism, prophets, a new worldview, and a stiff distaste for the Establishment. Most of these movements are rooted in obvious and serious crises, and frequently are part of a religious and political change in the culture.

The entire von Däniken affair, even much of the UFO interest associated with it, is, I think, very much like these movements. Only hindsight will give a good perspective on this point in American history, but the "we are not alone" attitude has become an important element of our culture's religious cosmology. A frustration with science's not having delivered all that it promised, a distaste for the specialization of scientific research, and a continuing need to believe in an intelligence beyond our own are the main characteristics of this anti-science mysticism.

It does not take much imagination to see that science has been, for many in our culture, the New Religion, with its white-frocked priests talking in strange tongues about a universe we couldn't even understand. (Try to grasp the idea of a boundless universe doubling back on itself, a la Einstein.) The priests' accomplishments in a few areas like technology and medicine were enough to satisfy the faithful.

But as a religion, science didn't stand the test of time. The contrast between what we could do in space with what we could do for ourselves on Earth was like watching a priest celebrate mass with his zipper down. Science is rather stale as a religion, and it cannot substitute for one. The man-in-the-street prefers a richer religion than that.

If von Däniken's thesis is part of your religious cosmology, so be it. I don't argue religion; I try to study it and see how it relates to human life. But if von Däniken seems like science to you, shame on you.

What follows is an attempt to lay open von Däniken's approach as a warped parody of reasoning, argumentation, as well as a vigorous exercise in selective quotation, misrepresentation, and error based on ignorance (presumably, if it is not intentional fibbing).

For students, his work does serve two valuable purposes: first, it raises their interest in the cultures and myths he so badly mishandles; and second, like Lewis Carroll's *Alice in Wonderland*, *Chariots of the Gods* is a challenge to study and determine all that is wrong with it. So it is by no means a complete waste of one's time (either his, yours, or mine).

Briefly stated, *Chariots of the Gods* proposes that scientists have overlooked, or refused to inform the world of, the many pieces of evidence that suggest we have been visited, probably several times, by intelligences from other planets. Von Däniken argues that an open-minded approach to the ruins of past cultures, and their art and myths, raises many unanswered questions that can best be answered by accepting the hypothesis of extraterrestrial visitors.

Data from Incan, Mayan, Sumerian, Egyptian, and many other cultures that suggest the hypothesis include cave painting, architectural and technological accomplishments, and mythological events of great similarity around the world. Von Däniken says that the explanations given by scientists are too smug, and now that space travel is possible for us, we must at least admit that his hypothesis is as viable as anyone else's.

Some of my professors used to tell me that hypotheses are a dime a dozen; people make them up all the time. Making a hypothesis is not science; it's what you do with a hypothesis that more or less is science and is to be judged by others. Von Däniken is entitled to his hypothesis. But what does he do with it?

Argumentation is an art that can easily be perverted. One technique to make yourself sound good is the straw horse: misrepresent the thing you wish to argue against. Von Däniken's characterizations of archaeology and anthropology – fields that focus on precisely the kind of data he studies – are abysmal.

By denying the breadth of these fields and the wealth of data in them, he has left somewhat of a vacuum into which to float his own ideas, which are clearly not based on any background in archaeology or anthropology. These are not the only disciplines he chops. His critics are nearly unanimous in accusing him of misrepresenting or failing to understand even the rudiments of geology, mythology, psychology, chemistry, astronomy, and physics.

His technique is successful in part because there are many presumably educated people who don't understand these fields, or even the ways of scientists in general. He has played to the prejudices and stereotypes of those who are not scientists. The tone of "you and I, dear reader" places him and his readership in an underdog position against the monolithic "Establishment" of picky pedants who represent the scholars.

Another technique that works well for misleading the mind is the red herring. The object is to confuse the reader by introducing an extraneous issue so that he will not catch you on your main point. Politicians might introduce Motherhood and Apple Pie, but von Däniken has his reflections on truth, atomic war, and propagandizing for space research. Such comments are quite irrelevant to his arguments, and serve only to glaze the reader's critical judgment.

One final technique that is useful in argumentation is to warn the reader in advance about the criticisms that will be leveled by one's opponents. This is not the same thing as dealing with those criticisms, but neatly puts the critic on the defense when listeners say, "Aha! Von Däniken said you would say that!" thus somehow scoring a point for the home team.

What most depresses my fellow anthropologists and me is the way people accept von Däniken's unnecessarily anthropocentric and ethnocentric views of other people in the world and in history. Anthropocentricism is the assumption that other living, sentient, or intelligent creatures must feel and think or evolve as humans do. Ethnocentricism is the even more narrow assumption that other people must think, behave, or evolve as we do. Further, there is usually a heavy flavor of cultural superiority in such assumptions.

Chariots of the Gods plays upon most people's inability to break out of these assumptions. It implies that up until the last thousand years or so, the world was filled with primitives, heathens, savages, and dummies. Their intelligence matched their simple technologies; their languages were simple, their cultures were primitive, and they were brutes.

If they seem to have come up with something quite fantastic by our standards, someone smarter than them must have given it to them. Von Däniken's reasoning, conservatively stated, is: there are some real mysteries in the past, because it is obvious that people who lived then are not solely responsible for those remarkable things. There are indeed real mysteries in the past, but they are usually not the ones von Däniken sees.

When one consciously puts aside the prejudices of his own culture and examines the cultures of the peoples mentioned in *Chariots of the Gods*, one begins to see the way myth, art, architecture, politics, kinship, and technology relate to one another, reflect and react to one another. The "fit" of many of these seemingly bizarre practices in the rest of their culture is often, in itself, a wonder to behold.

Von Däniken's book is a virtual goldmine of logical fallacies, implications by innuendo, and rhetorical questions, and failures to apply "Occam's Razor." Alicia Ostriker, who interviewed von Däniken for *Esquire*, wrote, "So what if the fallacies fly by in flocks like mallards heading south?" She was captivated by the man's enthusiasm and chose to overlook his "gee-whiz style, fit only for kiddies." She chose to overlook his flaws, but many other people *don't see them*.

A non sequitur, or logical fallacy, makes a conclusion that does not follow from the premise. The book starts out with a few non-sequiturs. On page vii, von Däniken argues that if you ignore his book, then you are a layman who refuses to face the adventurous and mysterious past.

On page two, he says that if one accepts the possibility of developed life elsewhere in the universe, then it must have been a civilization. Here is an example, from page 28, phrasing the main thesis of the book: "Since we are not prepared to admit or accept that there was a higher culture or an equally perfect technology before our own, all that is left is the hypothesis of a visit from space!"

A rhetorical question places the entire burden of proof on the reader, who either acquiesces because of the generally bewildering style of the argument, or passes the burden of proof on to the "scholars." When contemplating the ruins of Tiahuanaco, in Bolivia, von Däniken writes, on page 21: "Had our forefathers nothing better to do than spend years – without tools – fashioning water conduits of such precision?"

Applying Occam's razor means that when two explanations for one set of facts are possible, one adopts the simplest explanation – that is, the one that assumes the least number of "ifs." Von Däniken has argued that space travel is a simple explanation, since it is now possible by us.

However, it is not the possibility of space travel or of extraterrestrial intelligence that is questionable. The thesis of *Chariots of the Gods* fails by Occam's razor, because it constructs a gigantic house of cards, each card requiring a new "if." The "ifs" are held together by faith alone, and patently contradict most of the principles "science" had begun to see as a rather unified system.

Look, for example, at von Däniken's thesis that modern humans are the act of deliberate breeding by extraterrestrial intelligences. The fossil record of humanlike creatures and the culture they possessed stretches back more than a million years. Through the millennia, by rather gradual steps, we see the body approaching modern shape and the brain approaching modern size.

Cultural developments like fire, sophisticated stone tools, burials, tailored clothing, and so forth appear long before modern Homo sapiens. To see ourselves as a continual development of those trends, moving and adapting to the changing climates, creatures, and contours of the land, is much tidier than introducing some undefined, undated appearance of superior "breeders."

Von Däniken plays heavily on the reader's readiness to conclude that a long string of random possibilities equals a certainty. By the same reasoning, it is a virtual certainty that you will get six heads in six coin tosses, since there is a real possibility (50 percent, to be exact) that one toss will come up heads.

Last, and perhaps most disturbing, is von Däniken's misrepresentation of the very process of "doing science." He does not exhibit, nor does he anticipate in the reader, any real facility in the nature of a "fact," an hypothesis, developing a theory, and proof (or more accurately, demonstration).

At one point (p.66), von Däniken disclaims that he is compiling a sequence of proofs of prehistoric space travelers: "that is not what I am doing. I am simply referring to passages in very ancient texts that have no place in the working hypothesis in use up to the present."

In other words, he doesn't know what a working hypothesis is, nor is he embarrassed to stamp "QED" on an enormous gaggle of tautologies (assume something, create an hypothesis, test, claim to have proved your assumption).

He avoids ever stating anyone else's explanation in reasonable terms. He is loose with his concept of proof, with which he bludgeons unidentified others for not producing. More than any other characteristic, it is this blithely ignorant toying with the method of scientific reasoning that marks the book's shabbiness.

JUST PLAIN WRONG

A review of *Chariots of the Gods* in *Book World* says, "To check his 'facts' would take months of research, since he never cites his authorities." His highly selective choice of what to introduce as data follows absolutely no discernable criteria. His translations make critics howl (with glee if they have a sense of humor, with rage if they do not).

Many of the "facts" and "questions" von Däniken presents have been checked out, and have been found wanting. For instance, he relies heavily on the Piri Reis maps (p. 14). While they are, indeed, amazing maps, they are far from accurate.

The mysteries he sees in the Tiahuanaco culture of Bolivia and the Sumerians could easily be clear up by reading Lanning, Braidwood, and Adams.

"Isn't there something rather absurd about worshipping a 'god' whom one also slaughters and eats?" he asks (on p.33). Actually, the answer is "no." The world has a number of people who do so: the Australian Aborigines, Mesopotamians, Ainu, and others.

Regarding the copper furnaces at Ezion Geber (p.44), he gives the wrong dates, and misses the obvious – that the rooms are storage rooms.

As to the "breeding experiments of space travelers on prehumans" (p.52), it defies all the principles of genetics and evolution. In *Gods From Outer Space*, he calmed down on this issue, but the book didn't sell, so he went back to it again in later books. The interviewer for *Esquire* magazine pointed out that von Däniken doesn't even seem to believe this stuff himself. If, so, then why say it? Answer: money.

For someone with such an interest in money, it is odd that his math is so bad when discussing things like the Cheops pyramid. And does the "suddenness of Egypt," according to Egyptologists (p.74), really lead us to suspect "someone put it there?" No. In fact, Egypt developed out of a Neolithic farmer culture a thousand years after civilization began in Mesopotamia.

On page 84, he asks, "Did the Egyptians learn the possibility of mummification from nature? If that were the case, there ought to have been a cult of butterflies or cockchafers. But there is nothing of the kind." Wrong again. Worship of the scarab beetle, the ibis, and other animals was widespread, and many were mummified.

On the terra cotta heads made in Jericho ten thousand years ago, he declares: "That, too, is astonishing, for ostensibly this people did not know techniques of pottery making" (p.87). This is wrong on several counts, one being that terra cotta had been made into statues for over ten thousand years before that date.

He gets his eras mixed up, too: "I would suggest, on tolerably good grounds, placing the incident I am concerned with in the Early Paleolithic Age – between 10,000 and 40,000 B.C." (p.88). In fact, the Early Paleolithic ended about 200,000 years before that. What he is describing is called the Upper Paleolithic and Mesolithic.

He wonders how a "Chinese" jade necklace found its way to Guatemala on page 93. This one threw me for a minute, but Clifford Wilson says jade is indigenous to Central America.

He claims that in Christ's day, "the concept of a heaven with fixed stars taking into account the rotation of the earth did not exist" (p.105). But to quote Ostriker: "What the average reader of von Däniken probably doesn't know is that the idea of life on other worlds is not exactly a new one." She further points out that before Ptolemy's geocentric worldview came along, a number of cultures were not far off from the view we hold now.

Von Däniken questions the drawings of "animals that simply did not exist in South America ten thousand years ago, namely camels and lions" (p.106). But it could be that these are simply llamas and pumas, which are native to the area.

Similarly, he claims there are "artificially produced markings, as yet unexplained, on extremely inaccessible rock faces in Australia, Peru, and

Upper Italy" (p.106). Speaking just for Australia, the aborigines have been seen to make the same markings in their totemic rituals. Obviously, the same could be possible in other places.

He makes a big deal about engravings of cylindrical rocketlike machines in Kunming, China (p.107), but this is a no-brainer, since the Chinese invented gunpowder and shot rockets!

These are just some of the items I caught. Others, like rustless iron columns in India, the Easter Island stones, and so forth are not quite the mystery von Däniken claims.

This review has been aimed at those readers of von Däniken who feel that in the interests of science and reasonableness, we should consider his argument. I have sketched some of the reasons why, when one considers his argument, one discovers no science or reasonableness in it.

The mass popularity of *Chariots of the Gods* doesn't derive ultimately from any interest in science or reasonableness but, as I have suggested, stems from a reaction *against* science and reasonableness. There is some justification for such a reaction. I myself advocate a dose of insanity in everyone's life, and von Däniken's book is a good read if you need a dose of enthusiastic delirium. However, I do not mix my insanity and my science.

CHAPTER 6

ERICH VON DÄNIKEN'S *CHARIOTS OF THE GODS*: SCIENCE OR
CHARLATANISM? – ROBERT SHEAFFER – 1974

Was God an ancient astronaut? Do centuries-old legends of gods and heroes
tell of space travelers who came to earth from distant parts of the cosmos?
Are some of the ruins of antiquity remnants of great airfields, the favored
landing sites of extraterrestrial craft?

"Yes!" writes Erich von Däniken in his runaway bestselling book, *Chariots
of the Gods*. This phenomenally successful book is now in its forty-fourth
printing, with over four million copies currently in print. Von Däniken's
sequels to this book, *Gods from Outer Space* and *The Gold of The Gods* are
also selling well, as are flocks of imitations.

The popularity of such a sensational theory should not be surprising.
Immanuel Velikovsky created a similar stir almost 25 years ago with the
publication of his *Worlds in Collision*, suggesting that the present state of the
solar system can be explained by a series of spectacular cataclysms among
the planets.

It has been over 27 years since "flying saucers" burst into the public's
awareness, and UFOs still continue to generate excitement and controversy.
Sensational hypotheses such as these generate such levels of interest that
they tend to become self-sustaining, quite apart from the question of
whether they are true.

Established science has always shied away from such remarkable claims. "It
took courage to write this book, and it will take courage to read it," says von
Däniken. "Even if a reactionary army tries to dam up this new intellectual
flood, a new world must be conquered, in the teeth of all the unteachable,
in the name of truth and reality."

(Presumably the reader here is expected to shout, "Right on!") Does science
avoid von Däniken because it is afraid to face up to the truth? Let's examine
some of his many claims, to see if they are serious scientific theories, or mere
humbug.

On page 9, von Däniken serves up a "basic rocket equation," derived by
one Professor Ackeret, purporting to show how time slows down for space
travelers who zip along at velocities near the speed of light. This is an
important consequence of Einstein's theory of relativity.

Yet, a quick glance at this "rocket equation" shows that it isn't an equation at all! Every equation is a mathematical statement of the equality of two quantities: this equals that. But his "equation" contains no equal sign, and hence it cannot be a real equation; it must be intended as window dressing, since it serves no legitimate mathematical purpose.

Yet that is not the only absurdity in this non-equation. A term in the denominator is multiplied by a very strange constant: one! Did Professor Ackeret think that multiplication by one was a necessary step in his calculations? Von Däniken himself must have known better, as even schoolchildren learn that any number times one equals itself! There are, of course, many legitimate equations that deal with this aspect of the relativity of time. Why then has von Däniken selected such an obvious humbug to support his "scientific " claims?

What is the history of our earth-moon system? Von Däniken claims, "A satellite was captured by the earth. As it was pulled toward the earth, it slowed down the speed of the earth's revolutions. It finally disintegrated and was replaced by the moon."

Proof of this theory, he writes, can be found in the symbols on the Great Idol in the Old Temple at Tiahuanaco, one of his favorite archaeological wonders. Supposedly this message, dating back 27,000 years, tells of how this satellite emeritus made 425 revolutions around the earth a year, which was then only 288 days.

If the earth formerly circled the sun every 288 days, Kepler's third law implies that the earth must have been at that time much closer to the sun, almost where Venus is now. Are we expected to believe that during the great Ice Ages, the earth was some twenty million miles closer to the sun than it is today?

On the other hand, if the year remained unchanged but each day is shorter, we are faced with another difficulty: since the year is now 365 days, the earth's rotation is faster than in 25,000 B.C., not slower as von Däniken claims. How could a satellite slowly spiraling earthward pull both Earth and satellite farther away from the sun? Where are the fragments of this disintegrated moon, and where did our current moon come from? Von Däniken gives no answers.

On ancient Egyptian astronomy, von Däniken asks, "Why a Sirius calendar? If Sirius appeared on the horizon at dawn at the same time as the Nile flood, it was pure coincidence… This very interest in Sirius seems rather peculiar, because seen from Memphis, Sirius can be observed only in the early dawn, just above the horizon, when the Nile floods begin."

Reader, beware – we're dealing with one who knows the art of deception!

Sirius, he neglects to mention, is the brightest star in the sky. His claim that Sirius was hardly visible at all to the Egyptians is simply false. Sirius, in fact, is visible from anywhere on Earth, except the extreme North Polar Region, and observers in Egypt see that star higher in the sky than we do here in the northern United States, where it dominates the sky on crisp winter evenings.

There is no dark mystery behind the development of the Sirius-based calendar in Egypt. The priests there noticed a simple regularity: each year, when that brilliant star first became visible in the morning sky, the Nile flood began. Does this not prove that the Egyptians had contact with a race of space travelers?

On the mysteries of the Great Pyramid of Cheops, von Däniken observes: "Is it coincidence that the area of the base of the pyramid divided by twice its height gives the celebrated figure Pi = 3.14159?"

Here, our slippery trickster has made a claim that is easy enough to understand, but its refutation requires a higher level of mathematical sophistication (which is all the better for letting the deception go unnoticed). Without going into too much detail, let us observe that the famous number Pi is what is called a "dimensionless constant": it is a pure number, with which no units of measure are associated. However, the ratio of an area to height is not dimensionless, hence such a ratio cannot yield Pi.

By choosing our units carefully, we can obtain the number 3.14159, but the ratio will not really be Pi, which is independent of any units of measure. If we measure the same pyramid, von Däniken style, in inches, feet, and yards, we will obtain three different ratios. Choose your own units, and the ratio can be made to equal any number at all! Von Däniken writes that the pyramid of Cheops "has inspired hundreds of crazy and untenable theories." Not satisfied with this collection, he has given us one more.

He offers more "evidence" of the ancient visitors: "The Mayas were intelligent; they had a highly developed culture. They left behind not only a fabulous calendar, but also incredible calculations. They knew the Venusian year of 584 days."

This statement is true – almost. He conveniently forgets to tell us that this 584-day period is not the true Venusian year (it is 225 days). Instead, it is the apparent Venusian cycle as seen by an earth-based observer, which is precisely what we should expect the ancient Mayas to record by simply counting days, without any extraterrestrial insight. On the other hand, if they had recorded the true Venusian year of 225 days, which implies a knowledge of the Copernican (sun-centered) system of astronomy, that would have been a bit more remarkable.

In these few short pages, I have scarcely begun a list of the inaccuracies and half-truths to be found in *Chariots of the Gods*. But a thousand-page refutation of a hundred-page book would hardly make good reading. Sensationalist theories have always attracted more readers than refutations of the same.

Enough of Von Däniken's claims have, however, been examined to reveal his method of operations: to dazzle the reader with a skillful blend of half-truths, quarter-truths, and eighth-truths. Looking into his past, we should not be too surprised to find that his rather broad criterion of truthfulness has, at times, brought him into conflict with the law.

A court in his native Switzerland found von Däniken guilty of embezzlement, forgery, and fraud, sentencing him to three and a half years in prison. While operating a Swiss hotel, it seems he fraudulently obtained money by misrepresenting his financial assets. This experience in deception later proved invaluable in his literary career. It was during this stay as a guest of the Swiss government that he wrote his second book, *Gods from Outer Space*, now also a bestseller.

Once a liar, however, does not prove him always a liar. However much this charlatanism may hurt one's credibility, it never destroys it completely. (The followers of famous psychics are never shaken when their leader is caught cheating: the "explanation" is that they only cheat on bad days!)

Von Däniken isn't just a researcher. He is also an experiencer or "contactee." In an exclusive interview with *The National Enquirer* in March 1974, Von Däniken told of his experiences in Point Aleph, "a sort of fourth dimension" where time doesn't exist. He revealed how he can now leave his body at will, transcending all concepts of space and time.

"I know that astronauts visited the earth in ancient times," he confides, because "I was there when the astronauts arrived. And I know they'll be back." Unfortunately for us, he can't say exactly when, since "time doesn't exist in Point Aleph."

"I even know what will happen after death," he claims. We're all ears. "I will become part of this huge, never-to-be-destroyed ball of energy that keeps and remembers every last tiny thing that has ever happened on this planet. Everybody will join me there eventually, and at least they'll know then that I was right."

Save a place for me right in the middle of that big old ball, Erich, because I'm going to be one of the hardest to convince.

CHAPTER 7

AUTHOR STICKS BY ET THEORIES: INTERVIEW WITH ERICH VON DÄNIKEN – FLORIDA TODAY (BILLY COX) – 1996

At age 62, the godfather of the Ancient Astronauts Society (AAS) may seem like a flawed relic from the 1960s. But Erich von Däniken never went away. Von Däniken has never wavered from his premise that ancient scribes writing in holy texts (in Eastern and Western traditions) were describing contact with technologically sophisticated extraterrestrial visitors.

Two weeks ago, production crews finished filming yet another documentary on the Swiss author's controversial research, which will air in the United States on the A&E Channel late this year or early 1997.

On a rain-soaked weekday afternoon inside Barnes & Noble Booksellers, a small but avid line of fans gathers for autographs of his 22nd book, *Return of the Gods*. Some offer dog-eared copies of von Däniken's groundbreaking first effort, *Chariots of the Gods*, translated into English in 1972. Since then, von Däniken's books have sold more than 53 million copies in 28 languages.

What only the most hardcore Von Dänikenites know is that the writer who, in the 1960s, began advocating extraterrestrial influences on world religions, culture and architecture, penned a mea culpa in 1985, entitled *Habe Ich Mich Geirrt?* Never translated into English, *Did I Get It Wrong?* is a retraction of some of his most falsifiable assertions involving ET artifacts that weren't.

Von Däniken is in Central Florida this week for the annual AAS meeting, being held in Orlando. *Florida Today* managed to get a few moments with the expansive and ostensibly tireless world traveler.

Florida Today (FT): Why are we seeing such an intense interest in the subject of extraterrestrials now?

Erich von Däniken: It's a complicated story. I think, thousands of years ago, some extraterrestrials created, by deliberate mutation, our intelligence. This does not contradict Darwin's theory of evolution. But it's just one step forward. If you would accept this as a theory, that we have some extraterrestrial genes in us, then these genes may one day grow and open.

If you have a tree with fruits, at a certain time the fruits ripen, and they fall off the tree. The fruit is the message of the extraterrestrials. At a certain time for humanity, the knowledge will come into our brain.

So why, now, is there more and more interest in extraterrestrials? In my opinion, it's because we have it in our genes. The time is right. You cannot stop the interest. It is growing and growing. It has nothing to do with the year 2000. The millennium has only to do with Christianity. The other societies – the Jewish community, the Islamic community, etc. – have different calendars altogether.

FT: How does this not conflict with Darwinism?

Darwin's theory of evolution is something that we learn and we generally accept. We have the bones and family trees that show that we basically come from apes. But apes are still primitive today. We are the only ones from this tree who have become intelligent. Why only we? Because, I say, we are a deliberate mutation made by extraterrestrials. Or as the religious texts say, the gods created man after their own image.

FT: You take a lot of swipes at fundamentalist interpretations of ancient texts. Why do you enjoy this process so much?

Because I am a deep believer in God. I am one of these people who still prays every day. God has to be timeless. A god who has to create experiments and wait for the results cannot be God. God has to be all-present. He does not need a vehicle in which to move around – a vehicle with smoke and fire and thundering. God, naturally, does not make any mistakes.

If you read the Bible, you find a god who is driving around in chariots, which the prophet Ezekiel describes very clearly. Or you find that God makes mistakes. According to the Bible, God created, in five days, the earth, the plants, and the trees, and on the sixth day, He made Adam and Eve. And then, according to the Bible, God said it was good.

But shortly after, He decided it was not good, because he decided to destroy humanity with a great flood. So I think these people (fundamentalists) are not praying to the real God.

FT: Are you saying they're stupid?

No, not stupid, just educated in this flaw. I myself am educated as a Catholic. And, naturally, I was a deep believer in the way of God as I was educated. But later, I realized some of the descriptions in the Old Testament could not be accurate descriptions of God. God is much bigger, and indescribable.

CHAPTER 7: AUTHOR STICKS BY ET THEORIES: INTERVIEW WITH ERICH VON DÄNIKEN

FT: So the early accounts got it all wrong?

The first gospels weren't written down until 40 years after the death of Jesus Christ. And the later gospels weren't even eyewitness to what happened. But the later stories went into that time, because, like all other times, it too was a political time. And the family of (Holy Roman Emperor) Constantine and his wife created a new religion (in 300 A.D.), which became Christianity.

It was a wonderful story, you know, Jesus Christ, the Son of God, finally ascended to heaven. Long before Christianity, there were many gods in other traditions who went to heaven. So naturally, Jesus had to ascend as well. In reality, the ascension never took place. The resurrection never took place. At least not like depicted in the Bible. The tomb of Jesus is in Kashmir. I have photographed it many times.

FT: Why do we need the ET factor to make us realize we're all from the same seed of life?

We don't necessarily need the ET factor, but it's helpful. Looking from the outside at this planet helps us realize we're all from the same place. What if the astronomers announced that there is something artificial out there? What would happen? We would immediately understand that all intelligent beings on this planet are one race – not blacks, whites, or whatever – and it makes no sense to make war.

FT: So if an announcement of that type would have this positive, unifying effect, why do you suppose – given the growing body of evidence we have on UFOs – it hasn't happened?

Our society is not only composed of the few people who make the government. Our society is much more complicated. You have very strong power in religion, very strong power in science, and in many other fields of society. And all these parts would be against UFO disclosure.

They don't want to have a loss of orientation. If there is a change in thinking about extraterrestrials, it should not happen by revolution, by fighting each other – people saying, "We are right, and you are the idiots." It should go by evolution, slowly, via the passing of two or three generations. Because they have a responsibility to society.

FT: Do you think that's what we're watching now? Culturally? A slow acclimation?

Yes. In my short life, I have had a very curious experience. I learned that we have two types of human beings. One type is educated scientifically. They absolutely believe in evolution, mutation, and selection. But on the end of this process of evolution, we are the greatest – the top of evolution.

The other type of person is educated in a religious way. They believe in the concept of God having created all this – on the sixth day, He created Adam and Eve, etc. But we are still at the top of creation, because God made us, finally. So it doesn't matter whether you look at it in a scientific or religious manner. In both cases – the top of evolution or the crown of creation – we are the greatest.

We don't like extraterrestrials. We don't want extraterrestrials; we are afraid of them. It's a psychological problem; we are not ready to accept that we are not the greatest.

FT: One of the criticisms is that your ET theories short-sell our own imaginations – our own creativity.

That's rubbish. Carl Sagan and the others who've attacked me, I'm sure they have never read my books. Naturally, it's nonsense to believe that any extraterrestrials created any buildings on Earth. Of course, our ancestors created these wonderful temples and pyramids. Our ancestors developed the culture, the religion. But the question still has to be answered: for what purpose?

I believe, thousands of years ago, ETs were here. Maybe only a small group of people saw them. They were interpreted as powerful gods, descended from heaven. The next generation never saw them, and never understood what they were.

The Maya, for instance, created incredible pyramids in Central America. You have to ask the Maya, "Why have you done these pyramids?" For the gods? What gods? Scientists say for the gods of nature, thunder, lightning – the strong forces they admired, but could not understand. But that's rubbish. Those natural forces do not speak.

The Maya, for example, explain that Kukulkan gave them astronomical knowledge and mathematics. I'm sorry, but lightning or some other natural force does not speak, "Divide this by this to get that," and so forth.

FT: Let's talk about the sarcophagus lid of King Pacal in Palenque – the idea of him being at the control panel of a spaceship. Isn't there enough ambiguity in this baroque avalanche of hieroglyphics to say that what has been described as flames and rocket exhaust could also be flowers, as the traditional Mayanists contend?

In our century, we have learned a new cult appeared. It's called the cargo cult. Whenever a high-technological society comes into contact with a primitive society, the primitives believe that some of the technology of the higher society is magic. If they can't understand it, it must have something to do with gods.

When Christopher Columbus arrived in the New World, the natives believed he was a god – at least in the beginning. When Francisco Pizarro showed himself to the Inca, with his chains glittering in the sun, the priests all fell on the ground, believing him to be the son of the sun.

In World War II, in the Pacific, on the island of Bebak, there were still Stone Age people who had never seen an aircraft. Then they saw these things landing on the coast. They went back to the mountain and began creating aircraft made of wood and straw. And they adored these models they made. It was magic. This is what we call the cargo cult – misunderstanding technology.

The extraterrestrials studied the people, and maybe gave some of the people information. And one of the priests tries to chisel this ET and his vehicle into stone. The man understands nothing of the technology, like the people on the island of Bebak who don't know what an aircraft was. He chiseled what he saw.

Today, there are nine different explanations for this Palenque figure in the books. They tell us it is the tomb of Pacal, the dynasty that ruled Palenque, and according to the inscription, this ruler should be the second to last Pacal. On the other side of the temple, we have datings of Pacal.

But the oldest date does not correspond to what we know about the Maya. It's translated to 3114 B.C., the very beginning of the Maya calendar, but long before the Maya appeared. So let's look at it in terms of misunderstanding technology, which is what we see today in our cargo cults. It's just a suggestion.

FT: You've made it easy for your critics, due to the time you spent in jail for fraud and embezzlement.

But that's all rubbish. I was found guilty of tax fraud in 1971 or '72. It took years and years until the case went to the Swiss federal court and then back again. It was overturned (in 1982) and I was found not guilty. Still, I had spent about 16 months in jail. It was terrible. You can do nothing. But years had passed, and I was not eager to bring it all up again. It's 30 years past.

I mean, if that's what they attack you for – for what happens in private –

then you cannot believe any politicians, certainly. And you couldn't even believe in Jesus (who was jailed, too). Forget it.

FT: How have your writings changed since "Chariots of the Gods?"

You learn that you make mistakes. In *Chariots of the Gods* are many things that I would never repeat again, because I was young. I was manager of a hotel at the time, and when you are young you are not self-critical enough, and you are enthusiastic. And you believe rubbish as the truth, and you write it down.

In *Chariots of the Gods*, I had something like 238 question marks. Nobody saw the question marks. Today, there are not so many.

FT: How about a prediction? What do you think Mars Global Surveyor or subsequent missions to Mars will find on Cydonia, where some people think there's a face and pyramids?

Well, I am definitely convinced they will find traces of life. Primitive life. The face on Mars? I was never convinced of that. I am not sure if that is a serious thing or not.

FT: Do you think NASA would play straight about discovering extraterrestrial intelligence?

No, not NASA – it is government science.

More than four years ago, a German engineer made this robot that goes into the (Giza) pyramid. It found a door to a chamber, 65 meters into a shaft. And why have Egyptologists not opened the door? Or if they have, why have they not published what they found? Why? It would be a sensation!

It has been said they are maybe afraid of exposing this to oxygen after all the centuries, but that's garbage. Because there is a corner on the bottom of the door that is missing. The door is not directly on the ground, because we see a laser beam that goes under and through the door, meaning oxygen has been coming in forever. So nothing happens. The question is, what's wrong with science?

In astronomy, we have one group of astronomers that work in the Search for Extraterrestrial Intelligence program (SETI). Well, at the last SETI conference, the honest and serious astronomers looking for radiowaves coming from outer space decided on self-censorship. If one of them finds what he is looking for, he is not allowed to publish. He has to contact this circle of scientists, and this circle, and this circle. Why? Where's the freedom of information?

FT: Maybe they're trying to protect their Nobel Prize.

OK. But why then is the same community attacking us for saying they are hiding something? I'm sorry, but they are hiding something; or will be. Look at the Dead Sea Scrolls. Why have scientists working on the Dead Sea Scrolls shut their mouths for more than 20 years? Something is going on there.

FT: Do you think you'll live to see a confirmation of your work?

No. I would have to be very lucky for that to happen. Even if someone could find an object definitely not of this planet, and they could give it to the scientific communities, I'm sure it would take much too long for this society to accept that extraterrestrials exist.

I have merely started something. There are 56 million copies of my books worldwide. But now it is not just Erich Von Däniken. It is others, many others, as well. You cannot kill the idea anymore – never.

CHAPTER 8

In "Strange Stone Spheres" (Pursuit, Vol. 19, No. 4), Mr. Shoemaker discussed in some technical detail existing information and present theories regarding the origin and possible intended purpose of the nearly perfectly round, sculptured stone spheres found in Costa Rica. Dr. Stone and Dr. Lothrop independently investigated the massive objects there. Now, in this article, Mr. Shoemaker moves from Costa Rica to other countries where similar spheres have been found, and reports his findings to us.

MORE ON STONE SPHERES – MICHAEL T. SHOEMAKER – 1987

Stone spheres of such enormous size, perfection, and quantity are found nowhere else in the world. Some comparable balls do exist, however, at many locations. Both Dr. Stone and Dr. Lothrop listed these parallels without discussing them or drawing any conclusions. This neglect has inhibited the search for the spheres' purpose and meaning. The parallels actually tell us a great deal, including the probable origin of the sphere-sculpting tradition.

In considering these parallels, we run the risk of equating completely unrelated balls. This is especially true of the small balls, by which I mean those that can be held in the hand – say, 6 inches or less. Such balls could have been used for several purposes not connected with the larger balls: in games or divination, as weapons, or as tools for smoothing and grinding. But as we shall see, the bulk of the data suggests that there often is a link between the small and large balls, so I think this justifies considering all of them.

Deciding whether the parallels are the result of cultural diffusion, or of independent invention, is also problematic. Those balls found throughout Central America and Mexico could have resulted from direct or indirect trading contact with the Diquis culture. Those that are farther away are more likely to be examples of independent invention.

Many sites in Costa Rica have small and medium-sized spheres. The most interesting is at Papagayo, on the peninsula beside Culebra Bay, in northwestern Costa Rica. Between 800 and 1200 A.D., this region supported the Nicoya culture, an independent group of tribes whose language and tradition had southern roots. Nicoya pottery has been found in the Diquis delta, so trade between the two is a certainty.

At Papagayo, four large foundations for houses show identical characteristics that indicate a general style. They are circular and were constructed with uncut stones. Resting on peg bases, stone sculptures of a single jaguar head and of multiple alligator heads surround each foundation.

High-relief sculptures of columns (Dr. Stone called them "monoliths") are interspersed between the heads. (Similar decorative columns are found in the late Mayan architectural style.) Two or more medium-size stone spheres were found in close association with these sculptures. It is not clear whether two spheres were found at each foundation (making eight in all), or only two altogether. Nor are the spheres' precise locations clear.

One wonders whether these spheres once sat on the top of the columns. Such a decorative device is found at the entrance to many old mansions in Europe, where it derives from Medieval symbolism in which the orb represented "the Infinite and Perfect One," according to antiquarian Harold Bayley.

In any case, the association of spheres with animal heads points to a totemic significance. The heads are certainly totems serving as guardians of the houses, for we know that the Indians throughout Costa Rica had an animistic religion in which alligators and jaguars had a special place.

No real parallels are found in eastern Costa Rica, because the mountains were an effective barrier to cultural contact. Only crude balls used as smoothing or grinding tools were found at Las Mercedes, a plantation on an affluent of the Rio de la Reventazon. These are easily distinguishable because of their very small size and mediocre workmanship. Other small balls found in northeastern Costa Rica are considered slingshots.

The highland plains of the Cartago Province hold genuine parallels, however. The site of an ancient settlement was discovered on a coffee plantation at Orosi, about 18 miles southeast of San José, Costa Rica's capital. At the turn of the century, C.V. Hartman excavated several stone-lined graves and an oblong mound found in a grassy meadow surrounded by mountains.

The mound, about 12 feet high, stood beside a "courtyard" enclosure of ground-level stones. Treasure hunters had dug into it and uncovered seven stone balls, which discarded, lay scattered in the grass below. Hartman dug deeper into the undisturbed layer and, in the process, discovered ten more balls along with potsherds and charcoal. He also found a skeleton in another part of the mound.

The largest balls had diameters ranging from 6 to 12 inches. Hartman offered no explanation for them, but noted, "In several other localities in the Cartago Valley, similar stone balls have been found near the settlements of the ancient inhabitants." This area was occupied by the Guetar people, another distinct group of tribes contemporary with the Diquis culture.

The graves were undistinguished, but since the mound covered both a house site and a skeleton, it may be an example of a special memorializing custom. Perhaps when a chief or shaman died, a mound was raised over his house and body as a monument. We see again that spheres are associated with both house sites and death.

Large and small balls have also been found in Honduras, and were apparently brought there by the Lenca people. The Lencas may be either immigrants from Costa Rica who came during the early centuries A.D., or another colony from South America. They are different from the other Honduran tribes, and their language is closer to the Chibchan dialects of Costa Rica and Colombia than to the Mayan and Nahuatl languages of the north.

At Tenampua, 25 miles northeast of Tegucigalpa, the Lencas established a fortified village on a flat promontory overlooking the Comayagua River. Dorothy Popenhoe, who excavated the site, found numerous red sandstone balls in various places. Without giving an exact size, she said they were each nearly equal in size, fit into one's hand, and weighed about three to four pounds. She discovered a large concentration of them a third of the distance down the hillside. The balls had clearly been hurled in defense of the fort, either by hand or by sling.

Popenhoe, writing before the Diquis spheres were found, thought the balls had been naturally formed in a river bed, but admitted that the stone was not of local origin. This led her to make the lame suggestion that the balls had been transported from another area. But who would transport mere stones for throwing unless the stones had some added magical significance?

Knowing what we do today, it is probable that the stones were both carved and transported. Water action is not likely to produce such a large quantity of relatively uniform, sandstone balls. The sandstone would probably crumble completely, or cleave along planes.

An especially intriguing detail is the red color of the stone. Could it be that this was meant to symbolize blood, perhaps in the hope of magically drawing blood from the enemy?

Another Lenca site has also yielded spheres. Dr. Stone found a large stone sphere (no exact size was given) at Travesia, on the Ulua River, some 90 miles downstream from Tenampua. It rested on the right side of the terrace of the Temple of the Carvings, the most important building at the site. Smaller balls, similar to those at Tenampua, were found inside the temple.

Contact between the Lencas and the Mayas may account for two spheres found at the Mayan city of Benque Viejo. This city lies on the Belize River, in Belize (formerly British Honduras), near the Guatemalan border. The trip from Travesia to Benque Viejo is not far and can be made entirely by water, which was usually the easiest highway for travel in the ancient world.

At this city, J. Eric Thompson found two granite spheres that both had a diameter of 1 foot, 10 inches. Since there is no local source of granite, these spheres must have been made somewhere else. As we would expect of a diffused artistic tradition, these spheres were carved more crudely than the Diquis spheres. Thompson found them on an artificially leveled area, so he attributed an unspecified ceremonial purpose to them.

But given the likelihood that these spheres were imported, which is enhanced by the fact that no others have been found in the area, they may actually be nothing more than decorative souvenirs from a foreign land.

A single quartz ball, little more than an inch in diameter, was found in Chichen Itza when the Carnegie Institution excavated and restored the Caracol, the famous Mayan "observatory." This ball, too, could have come from trade with the Lencas. It is also possible that the Toltecs brought it from the west, where they in turn may have acquired it from the Pacific Coast Mixtecs.

The Toltecs conquered Chichen Itza in about 1000 A.D., and most of the buildings in the city were built after this time. The lower platform on which the Caracol stands is dated to 800 A.D., but the dating for the Caracol itself is later.

The astronomical aspects of the Caracol have long overshadowed an intriguing fact about the structure. Its foundation is actually a kind of layered cemetery. The lower platform has about twelve burials within its *embutido* (the earthen fill inside the platform). And about 24 burials are in the upper platform's embutido.

Other buildings adjoin these platforms, and form a single complex with the Caracol. In one of these, the West Annex, a quartz ball was found. The inner chamber of the West Annex has a dais with niches along the front base. Along with the ball, pottery fragments were found in these niches.

The ball is easily distinguished from the large quantity of stone beads found in the embutido graves. The beads are roughly round with a hole through the middle, but the ball is superbly spherical and lacks a hole. The ball was not naturally formed, for it shows signs of human workmanship.

No one has speculated on the purpose of the West Annex, but I would guess that it had a funerary purpose. Perhaps the body lay-in-state on the dais, while the niches held offerings to the dead.

A funerary connection is explicit for the rest of the Mayan spheres. Thirteen balls have been found at two sites that are only 30 miles apart in southwestern Guatemala. Although they span hundreds of years, all of the balls were found in graves.

At Zaculeu, four roughly spherical balls were found in some graves of the Atzan Phase (500-700 A.D.). They had been sculpted by pecking, and their diameters were 3.9, 5.5, 9.1, and 14.6 inches. A fifth ball, 2.4 inches wide, was found in a Chinaq Phase urn-burial (800-900 A.D.).

Woodbury and Trik, the archeologists who excavated the site, also noted that river-worn pebbles were occasionally found in bowls in Atzan Phase burials. They believed these pebbles were ritual offerings, and suggested that the smallest balls served a similar purpose.

Actually, the two larger balls are even more likely to have had a ritual significance, because they are too unwieldy to have had the ordinary practical uses that are often attributed to the smaller balls. The largest of these balls weighs 125 pounds.

Practical uses have indeed been attributed to the eight balls found at nearby Tajumulco, which is dated to 1000-1250 A.D. These balls are all small, with the largest only 5.6 inches wide. They were found in a tomb with grave goods including mortars and other tools, and several of them have flattened and abraded surfaces consistent with tool use.

Ironically, however, the one ball actually found in a grinding mortar had a very smooth surface that was not flattened. This does not sound like a tool, and its location in a mortar could be accidental. Two of the six mortars further confuse the question, for they have cavities that are too deep for use with a grinding ball.

Zaculeu and Tajumulco are close enough to the Pacific coast to have acquired sphere-sculpting directly from the south. But even if these spheres resulted from cultural diffusion, rather than from independent invention, the idea behind them obviously never became very popular.

The Olmec site of Cerro de las Mesas, fifteen miles east of the Bay of Alvarado, in Vera Cruz, has two of the largest spheres outside of Costa Rica. The site was apparently a ceremonial center, for it has the only stone monuments in the vicinity. These monuments were erected over a long period of time, probably by more than one culture.

Two spheres are among the monuments found on a stone plaza. One is slightly oblate, and the other rests on a flat spot reminiscent of Costa Rica's coquina spheres. Matthew W. Stirling, who described the site, did not give sizes, but a photo shows that these spheres are about the size of a machete, perhaps two feet in diameter.

These spheres are presumably the work of the Mixtecs, a people from Oaxaca who were eventually conquered by the Aztecs. The Mixtecs occupied this site at some late time, and erected groups of mounds throughout the area. Although the diffusion theory may apply to the Mixtecs, it is peculiar that no spheres have been found in Oaxaca, where we would most expect them.

Could sphere-sculpting have originated with the Olmecs (1200 B.C. – 0), as so much else in Meso-American culture did? Spheroid head-sculptures similar in size to the two spheres were also found at Cerro de las Mesas. These call to mind the Olmecs' famous, gigantic head-sculptures, which have a scale and general rotundity comparable to the Diquis spheres. Although the notion is rather fanciful, spheres could have been either the first stage of head-sculpting, or maybe an abstract style that grew out of head-sculpting.

Even if the Olmecs made spheres before the Diquis culture began, the tradition may still have derived from South America. Recent discoveries have shown that the bar-dot vigesimal system of mathematical notation, which was first attributed to the Mayas and then to the Olmecs, was really invented in the Andes.

There is also a possibility that the spheres at Cerro de las Mesas have an altogether different origin than the other spheres considered thus far. Depending on the type of rock that composes them – for Stirling did not identify their composition – these spheres may be either naturally formed, or else inspired by naturally formed spheres.

Several hundred naturally formed stone spheres lie on the slopes of the Sierra de Ameca, about 50 miles from Guadalajara, in Jalisco, Mexico. These spheres have diameters between 2 feet and 11 feet; but many of them are lopsided, and a few are even shaped like dumbbells (caused by the fusion of two spheres). Unlike the polished Diquis spheres, their surfaces are quite rough.

Dr. Robert L. Smith, of the U.S. Geological Survey team, examined the Jalisco spheres in 1968 and concluded that they "were formed during the Tertiary geological period, by crystallization at high temperatures in a matrix of hot ash-flow tuff."

Based on other ash-flows, it is supposed that volcanic glass composes

80% of the spheres' weight, while air pores account for more than half their volume. The discovery of a sphere still encased in consolidated ash confirmed this hypothesized formation process.

This process cannot explain the Diquis spheres, however, because according to Dr. Smith, "Granitic rock never occurs naturally in large perfect spheres." Moreover, the polished surfaces of the Diquis spheres, and of the other spheres in Central America, indicate human workmanship.

Although the Jalisco spheres may be related to those at Cerro de las Mesas, and may have inspired the Olmec heads, it is doubtful that they exerted any influence outside of Mexico. The Diquis spheres would still be mysterious, however, even if their creation was inspired by natural spheres, because their purpose would remain unknown.

Stone balls, most of them small, have also been found at numerous sites in the United States. Considering the general lack of larger spheres, most of the small ones probably served one of the practical purposes already mentioned.

Four Hopi mounds near the central Petrified Forest, in Arizona, have yielded some sandstone balls. These balls are small, but very spherical and well made. Walter Hough, who excavated them, said they were "probably used in games," but that is nothing more than a guess.

In the Burton Mound at Santa Barbara, California, many elongated spheroids were uncovered. They had a groove, for a rope, around their long axis, and had been used as sinkers for fishing lines. Also found were "several worked spherical stones" that lacked a groove. These balls were about 2 inches wide and made of gray sandstone. In contrast to the sinkers, they had a smooth surface and excellent rotundity. The excavator offered no explanation for them.

Gerard Fowke, in an 1891 survey of "Stone Art," classified many of the small spheres as "hammers" or "hammerstones." He said they "show every stage of work, from the ordinary pebble with its surface scarcely altered, to the highly polished round or ovoid ball." According to Fowke, they were used to fashion other implements and "were assigned to specified purposes when brought to a better finish or form." He gave as an example a superbly spherical granite ball from Ross County, Ohio.

Fowke's blanket classification is not satisfactory. While some deformed balls may have served as hammers, a polished spherical stone such as the Ohio ball could hardly have been a hammer unless it was never used. One of his observations is interesting, however. He said that the balls "seem to be of more frequent occurrence in the northern districts than in the southern states, though found everywhere." Unfortunately, he did not give a list of sites or numbers.

Fowke also reported two additional original uses for small spheres. The Shoshone and Ojibwa Indians made a weapon in which the balls were "wrapped in leather, attached by a string of two inches to a handle 22 inches long." And the Indians of Queen Charlotte Island, British Columbia, Canada, used "elaborately carved round stones, mounted in handles as clubs."

Most of the small U.S. balls seem to bear no relationship to the Diquis spheres. We have, however, one slight indication that some of them may have had an esoteric purpose. In *Prehistoric Man*, Daniel Wilson quoted (without reference) from the American Ethnological Transactions, in which the pioneering ethnologist Henry Rowe Schoolcraft described a stone ball from an unspecified Indian mound. The ball had a diameter of 1.4 inches, and a flattened circular spot with an inscription appearing on it. Wilson said the circle had a 0.8-inch circumference, but he undoubtedly meant a diameter of the circle.

Schoolcraft identified a Greek delta in this inscription, but that is ridiculous, I feel, since the symbol referred to is connected to a long stem. In truth, the inscription is indecipherable. The signs are probably magical, rather than alphabetic or arithmetic. The ball certainly must have had some special significance.

A few large spheres have also been found in the U.S., although there is some question about their authenticity. A.C. Nelson, of Palisade, Minnesota, described some in a 1952 letter to *Fate*. He reported that in Mandan, North Dakota, he had seen some "perfectly round" sandstone balls that had diameters of about 10 to 12 inches.

He was told that Cannonball, North Dakota, had similar stone balls, and that the balls had even inspired the town's name. Some people, probably referring to Indian legends, said that giants had made the balls, while others attributed the balls to the action of glaciers. Mr. Nelson made an acute observation when he said that "because of their round form and uniform size," he believed humans had made the balls.

J.S. Russell, of Orlando, Florida, wrote to *Fate* a few months later, insisting that such balls resulted from stones rolling down streams and rivers. He said he knew of many stone balls at Graysville, Tennessee, between Lone Mountain and the Cumberlands. Their diameters range from a few inches to 6 feet. He admitted, however, that some of them are not round. This leaves us wondering whether any of them are truly round, or whether Mr. Russell lumped together manmade spheres with water-rounded boulders.

Mr. Russell's letter is really irrelevant to the question of the North Dakota spheres. If these spheres have been accurately reported, they must be of human origin for the reason that Mr. Nelson stated.

The existence of at least one large sphere in the U.S. is supported by a more authoritative source. Jacob Green, writing in *The American Journal of Science* in 1822, described a rocking stone located on the farm of Mrs. McCabbe, of Phillips Town, Putnam County, New York. (This rock should not be confused with the more famous "Putnam Rock," which once stood on the Hudson Palisades near West Point.)

Mr. Green provided an illustration that shows a hemisphere that looks exactly like half an egg balanced somewhat off-center. The curved sides are perfectly smooth, but the "flat" side is very jagged, exactly as though a former sphere had broken in half. Mr. Green said the stone was granite and was 31 feet in circumference. It rested on a "pedestal" that rose 1.5 feet off the ground. The stone could "be rolled a little by the hand, and with a small lever, it can be moved with great ease; notwithstanding this, six men with crowbars have been unable to roll it down from its pedestal."

I have been unable to determine whether this stone still exists, but there is no reason to doubt that it once did. Britain, and many other countries, formerly had numerous rocking stones, a few of which can still be seen. According to Harold Bayley's *The Lost Language of Symbolism*, "The Celtic Clachabrath, or rocking-stones, where spheres of enormous size, balanced with such nicety that the slightest touch caused them to vibrate."

Uncut boulders served as rocking stones in Cornwall, where such a stone is called a "logan." Bayley says, "There is a town near Cambourne called Illogan, and the word logan seems to imply that the tilting-rock was regarded as *ii-og-an* ("Our Lord the Mighty One").

The rocking stones suggest the existence of an earth-magic cult, and may have been idols to an earth goddess. They may also be related to the practices of erecting dolmens (huge boulders resting on peg-stones), which served as grave markers and sometimes as commemorative monuments.

In Malta, we find the best example of small balls used either for a game or for a divination ritual. Some of the earliest and most colossal megalithic temples were constructed by an indigenous civilization on the Maltese archipelago.

The temple at Tarxien, built before 2200 B.C., has a stone kiosk that stands by an outside corner near the entrance. Small holes cover the kiosk floor, and stone balls, also found at the site, fit into the holes. The temple has within it several sculptures of fat women, believed to represent a fertility goddess, which is usually associated with the earth. So we see again a possible link between stone balls and a cult of earth magic.

Some spheres that can be eliminated from consideration should also be mentioned. In the Sahara, elongated, medium-size "balls" have been found at many sites, but these were used, and are still used, to grind grain. Small balls, probably used as weapons, have also been reported from Haiti and Puerto Rico.

We come lastly to South America in our search for parallels. Although it has never before been pointed out, the roots of the Diquis sphere-sculpting tradition, like the roots of almost all Diquis culture lie, I feel, in South America.

Throughout the Andes of Peru, Ecuador, and Bolivia, holy sites called huacas were formerly marked by cairns. The Spanish destroyed most of them, or erected crosses in their places, but some still remain. Each cairn held a large sacred boulder, or huancauri, on top. The huancauris are also referred to as *willka*, or *vilca*, stones. Willka meant "sun" in the old Quechuan language, and it had connotations of "ancestry," "lineage," and "descent."

This relationship between the sun and stone is not as puzzling as it may seem. The sun was the supreme object of worship – the giver of life – in the Andes. Because sparks can be produced when a stone is struck, it was believed that part of the sun resides in rocks. The Andean myth of human origin reinforced this relationship.

Kon Tiki Viracocha, the incarnation of the sun-god, is supposed to have fashioned the first man out of stone. Building on this myth, the Incan mythology said that three eggs (often symbolized by stones) descended from the sun and gave birth to the three districts of the Inca Empire. (The "ancient astronaut" school of interpretation regards this as a visitation by spaceships.)

The vilca stones were not in themselves worshipped. They held the spirits of the dead and acted as oracles. This comes close to a totemic function, and indeed, Villca is a tribal name, indicating that the vilca stones probably did serve as totems occasionally.

Willkapampa, known to us as Vilcabamba, meant "Plain of the Sun." Old Vilcabamba (to distinguish it from a modern town of the same name) was the famous "lost city" to which Manco II and the Incas retreated after Cuzco fell to the Spaniards. Machu Picchu was once believed to be Old Vilcabamba, but this was wrong. Explorer Gene Savoy discovered the true site in 1964.

Among the ruins, Savoy found an immense boulder that looked like an egg sitting on a platform. As more of the city was uncovered, huge uncut boulders were found everywhere. He then realized that Old Vilcabamba was literally a city of vilca stones.

In 1965, while exploring the Amazonas and San Martin provinces of northern Peru, Savoy discovered extensive ruins of the Chachapoyas culture (c. 800-1480 A.D.). At the ruins of Gran Pajaten, he found many circular, stone buildings, some as small as three feet in diameter. Some of these buildings contained pure white boulders shaped like an egg and as big as a basketball. These boulders were worshipped according to local tradition, and they can probably be likened to the vilca stones.

The Chachapoyas culture probably derived from the Chavin culture (c. 2000 B.C.). This provides a possible origin of the reverence for boulders, and one that is old enough to antedate the Diquis tradition. We will never know precisely where or when this practice began, but it clearly originated in the Andes, where it remained strong and widespread, and was exported to the Diquis delta, where it became a high art.

THEORIES AND CONCLUSIONS

Although the preceding paragraph foreshadows my general conclusions, a review of the theories about the spheres will strengthen and clarify my position. Ivan T. Sanderson, the late eminent zoologist and writer on scientific anomalies, first set forth the seven general purposes that the spheres could have served. The categories are: astronomical, mechanical, topographical, frivolous, artistic, economic, and religious.

The astronomical uses (sightlines or sky maps) are the most often proposed, but they are, ironically, the least likely. In fact, I think we can definitely rule them out. The forest and terrain make sightlines impossible and sky maps doubtful today and probably then, as well.

The size variations appear to have no special meaning (such as representing different star magnitudes), but probably reflect the sequence of production. If the balls formed sky maps, we would have to believe in several maps, some with only one or two balls, in order to explain their wide distribution. Most damaging are the positive clues – the associations with death and house mounds, and the evidence from Peru (which is absolutely inconsistent with the astronomical theory).

The mechanical theory includes using the spheres like steamrollers or as weights, either for weighing, or for storing potential energy. Most of the balls are too small to serve as rollers, and they would not be of much use in a flood delta. As weights for weighing, the large balls far exceed the Indians' requirements, for there is nothing that big to be weighed.

In an energy storage system, the balls could have been rolled up hills and released when needed. Such a system would offer the following advantages: control over time (like a battery), the accumulation of small amounts of force (if many balls are released together), and the steady application of an untiring force (in a ball's controlled descent).

Delivery of the energy would require some attachment such as an axle, however, and there is no evidence of any high-energy work having been done (except for sculpting and moving the spheres themselves). Furthermore, the positive clues do not support a mechanical explanation, either.

According to the topographical theory, the spheres could have been a system of boundary markers, or surveying tools that simplified the geometric calculations, but their distribution and range of sizes cast doubt on these uses. And an elaborate boundary system, with the markers often underwater, is hardly believable for a fishing culture such as that of the Diquis delta. And the positive clues contradict this theory, too.

Although sphere-sculpting probably involved artistic motives, it is not likely that the spheres were made to be primarily ornamental. Art generally evolves, but the sphere-sculpting appears to have continued unchanged for centuries. Nor is it believable that such a laborious art could have continued through the long period of warfare after 800 A.D.

A frivolous, or gaming, use of the spheres is not as outlandish as it sounds. The Tarahumara Indians of northwestern Mexico, for example, play a marathon kickball game that often covers up to 200 miles. Although we cannot disprove that these balls were pushed around in some kind of game, the religious explanation is far more convincing.

Seemingly the strangest of all is the idea that the spheres were a form of money. Large stone money – shaped like millstones – has been used in some Pacific islands. In fact, this form of money has several advantages over our own. It has an intrinsic value (the labor to produce it), it cannot be counterfeited, and it is virtually impossible to steal or to conceal (thereby eliminating tax evasion).

This theory offers an excellent explanation for the huge number of spheres, but there is no specific evidence in its favor, and it does not seem consistent with the existence of alignments.

Only the religious interpretation fits all the facts while remaining reasonable. Archaeologists (including Dr. Lothrop) have often suggested that the spheres had religious significance, but none has ever attempted to explain what that significance may have been.

It is ironic that Dr. Lothrop refused to believe the Boruca Indians when they told him that the spheres represented the sun. His reason was that the sun is usually symbolized in the New World by a gold disk (as we see among the Aztecs and Incas). But multiple symbols may have existed for a variety of reasons.

For example, the gold disks are valuable and rare; they would be suitable for the Emperor's priests, but hardly likely to be possessed by the poor mountain peasants. Or the disks may have been evolved symbols of later origin.

The Boruca Indians were indeed correct. As we have seen, the huancauris were vilca (sun) stones. Colonists apparently carried this tradition to the Diquis delta. Their attempt to perpetuate the tradition with river boulders and coquina proved unsatisfactory, so they began quarrying granite in the mountains. To them goes the credit for creating vilca stones that were perfect spheres. This development could have had an artistic or a philosophical motivation.

The association with death is perfectly natural. Sun symbols throughout the world are usually linked to the cycle of birth and resurrection, because the sun dies and is reborn daily. The spheres at the eastern and western boundaries of the Changuina cemetery are powerful examples of this symbolism.

As I have indicated, the vilca stones probably served as totems for some tribes in Peru. In the Diquis culture, the spheres appear to have been a tribal or supratribal totem – in other words, a totem that applied to everyone in the culture.

Archaeologists tell us that the Indians' religion was animistic (i.e., totemic), and the association between spheres and house mounds is also suggestive. The best supporting evidence comes from the Papagayo site, where spheres and totemic animal-heads were found together.

This interpretation accounts for the wide distribution and large number of spheres, and for the small spheres, too. Just as crucifixes are found in most houses of a Catholic country, so the spheres are found on the house mounds (upper class) and on the ground at stilt-house sites (lower class). And just as some people wear crosses, so the ancient Borucas may have carried with them the small spheres in pouches.

Some questions are still unanswered, of course. The psychology underlying such a prodigious and single-minded enterprise is hard to comprehend. Why are the rest of the Diquis sculptures so crude? Did the alignments have a magical significance?

Were the Old World dolmens similar to vilca stones; and if they were, did the idea spring from a fundamental of human consciousness, or from transatlantic diffusion? Unless we invent a time machine, these questions will probably remain forever beyond science.

CHAPTER 9

CHEROKEE LITTLE PEOPLE LEGENDS OF NORTH CAROLINA – RON MARTZ – 1988

On summer nights, when the moon is full and the sweet scent of honeysuckle is thick on the North Carolina mountains, Bessie Jumper believes she can hear the Little People drumming and dancing in caves in the rocky hillsides high above her home.

Mrs. Jumper, an aging Cherokee Indian who lives in the Snowbird Mountains near Robbinsville, North Carolina, does not venture into the woods. To look for the Little People, says Cherokee legend, is to look for trouble, and Mrs. Jumper does not want to risk the wrath of that race of elflike Indians known in the Cherokee language as *Yunwi Tsunsdi*.

When a non-Indian asked Mrs. Jumper about the Little People, she stared long and hard, as if to say that there are some things a white man should not ask an Indian. Then, without answering the question, she went back to stirring a pot of hominy that was cooking over an open fire.

In winter, when deep snow has buried the trails that run through the mountains, Cherokee hunters say it is not unusual to find small footprints that follow those unseen trails and lead them to safety. But to retrace the tiny, childlike footprints to where the Little People live is to risk being pelted by rocks or having a spell cast from which there is no recovery.

Many elderly Cherokees believe the Little People still live in these thickly wooded, remote mountains of western North Carolina. The Little People are not wraiths that glide through fogbound hollows in the dead of night or ethereal apparitions that rise with the moon and dance on the wind near the rocky promontories of Mount LeConte.

Nor are they the supernatural manifestations of overeager imaginations. Cherokees believe the Little People are a race of Indian spirits that predate man. They are the protectors of tribal tradition and the keepers of Cherokee history. They are revered, feared, and treated with the kind of distant respect with which one treats capricious spirits.

"There are many stories about the Little People, but most of the older people are afraid to talk about them, because the Little People can be good or bad. You never know," said Lois Calonehuskie, a Cherokee from Robbinsville and a frequent visitor in the Cherokee community of Snowbird, which is tucked into the shaded mountain hollows a few miles south of Robbinsville.

Cherokees escaping the Trail of Tears in 1838 fled into these thickly wooded, nearly impenetrable mountains of southwestern North Carolina, just a few miles from their ancestral homelands along the Little Tennessee River. They scattered throughout the mountains to evade capture, but eventually established their own community about 60 miles west of the main concentration of Cherokees (who refused to be moved to Oklahoma and hid out in the mountains around what is now Cherokee, North Carolina).

Martha Wachacha, however, said she didn't mind sharing some of the stories about Little People that she has been hearing most of her 77 years. Mrs. Wachacha, a pleasant, round-faced woman, sat on the banks of the Snowbird River with her hands folded in her lap and her eyes closed, as she talked about her days growing up in the mountains near Birdtown, North Carolina.

She told how she learned to weave baskets from thin splints of white oak when she was about 6 years old, and how she has been weaving baskets ever since. And she told of how late at night, when the whole family was working on baskets by the uncertain light of a kerosene lantern, her parents would tell stories about the Little People.

Mrs. Wachacha claimed she has never seen any of the Little People, but she has heard them laughing along creek banks. And she has heard their footsteps behind her at times when she was walking alone along mountain trails.

Mrs. Wachacha said the stories she heard of the Little People described them as about 1-1/2 feet tall, with perfect proportions and hair that touched their heels. Some wore gold caps, she said, while others wore nothing on their heads.

Gary Carden said the Little People are frequently confused with other Cherokee spirits that inhabit the surrounding mountains and rivers. Most notable among them are the Nunnehi, the "people who live anywhere" or "the ones who are always with us." The Nunnehi are immortal and invisible, except when they want to be seen, and they are usually portrayed as protectors of the Cherokee people.

"The Little People," said Carden, "are sometimes confused with the Nunnehi, but the Little People are more like the Welsh and Irish leprechauns. Most of the stories I have heard about them indicate that each Cherokee is born with a personal guardian who is one of the Little People. The Little People also help hunters, reveal lost items, and help with chores."

John Roth of Carlsbad, New Mexico, has spent several years chasing Indian spirits and legends across the country, trying to collect enough information for a book on the subject. Roth, a national park ranger, said he has at times had difficulty obtaining information from some tribes, because of a reluctance to share tribal mythology with non-Indian outsiders.

But Roth said he learned from Oklahoma Cherokees that Little People accompanied Cherokees from North Carolina on the infamous Trail of Tears. Finding no mountain caves in Oklahoma in which to live, the Little People learned to live in the deep holes in Tenkiller Lake and nearby creeks.

Mrs. Calonehuskie, a counselor at Robbinsville High School, said, "Sometimes at night, people will wake up and hear footsteps and voices in their houses. When they get up to see who is there, they find nothing. But in the morning, when they go to the kitchen and they find some food missing, they know the Little People have been there."

Other times, said Mrs. Calonehuskie, "You'll be standing by a stream and you'll hear children laughing, but, when you go to look, there's no one there. Then you know the Little People have been there."

There are also stories of Little People harvesting corn, clearing fields and chasing away burglars. The Little People are an integral part of Cherokee tribal history and mythology, and help enhance their spiritual reverence for the mountains they called *Shaconage*, "the place of the blue smoke."

According to one Cherokee legend, each fall, the spiritual leaders of the tribe would go to spires known as Chimney Tops, which are in the heart of what is now the Great Smoky Mountains National Park. The shamans, or medicine men, would stay there for seven days, praying to their spirits, retelling the legends of the tribe, and sharing what they had learned the previous year.

At nightfall on the seventh day, the Little People emerged from their caves and joined the Cherokees in singing and dancing. At dawn, the Little People filtered back into the forest, and the shamans returned to the tribe, spiritually enriched for another year.

But most stories that are told of the Little People concern their help to others. These stories are prevalent in James Mooney's 1901 book, *Myths of the Cherokee*, which is still considered the most authoritative ever written on the subject.

The book was reproduced in 1982 by Charles and Randy Eller of Nashville, Tennessee, and is available in many bookstores and gift shops in the mountains of western North Carolina. Mooney, an Indian agent, collected material for his book while living with the Cherokees from 1887 until 1890.

One story Mooney relates in his book tells of a hunter who found small tracks, like those of children, in the snow deep in the mountains. The hunter followed the tracks to a cave and found it full of Little People dancing and drumming, as they normally do. The hunter was taken in by the Little People, given a place to sleep, bread to eat, and he stayed with them for 16 days. The hunter's friends thought he had died in the mountains and stopped searching for him.

"After he was well rested," Mooney wrote, "they had brought him a part of the way home. They came to a small creek about knee deep, and they told him to wade across to reach the main trail on the other side. He waded across and turned to look back, but the Little People were gone, and the creek was a deep river. When he reached home, his legs were frozen, and he lived only a few days."

The Cherokees say it is important for anyone who walks through the high regions of the Smokey Mountains to remember that it is the home of the Little People.

CHAPTER 10

SKY GODS AND OUR SEEDED PLANET – JOHN A. KEEL – 1976

Swiss author Erich von Däniken has become an international celebrity because of his claim that mankind was first seeded on this planet by beings from another world. The gods of the ancients were, according to his theory, astronauts from some distant planet. In his latest book, von Däniken embellishes this concept by suggesting that all religious miracles and ghostly apparitions are projections and manipulations by that far off civilization.

Actually, the "seeded planet" theory has been bandied about in scientific and science fiction circles for a great many years. A host of European authors had produced massive volumes based on the theme long before Von Däniken picked up his pen. But none had managed to capture the public's imagination. Certainly, no one before Von Däniken had succeeded in raising so much public discussion and debate on the matter.

Is it possible – really possible – that the first man came to Earth from somewhere else? If so, how did he originate on that other world? Was he seeded there from still some other place? It's the age-old question of which came first, the chicken or the egg. Is the story of Adam and Eve in the Garden of Eden actually a description of another planet – another beginning?

That story did not begin with the *Book of Genesis*, but was part of the folklore of many ancient cultures. It told simply how the first man and woman found themselves stranded on an alien world – a world already occupied by a hostile force or group known as the "serpent people."

The serpent people did not appreciate the innocent intruders, and tried to get rid of them in all kinds of fiendish ways. Modern theology translated these serpent people into the Christian devil. The serpent was simplified into a symbol – a demonic creature that encouraged Eve to violate a cosmic secret: to eat the fruit of the sacred apple tree.

Some invisible super-intelligence was overseeing the situation, protecting Adam and Eve from the serpent people, but after they had broken the rules, they were cut off from direct contact with the super-intelligence, and all of our problems began. We have been trying to reestablish contact with the invisible overseer ever since.

We began with "magic," – with secret rites that sought communication with the overseer but which, more often than not, merely succeeded in stirring up the serpent people or demonic forces. As our population grew, we set up religions built around men who claimed they were in close contact with the overseer.

Many of the ugly rites of the earlier magical cults were cleaned up and adopted by later religions. In the West, we even adopted the pagan holidays as our own. Winter solstice became Christmas. The spring holiday devoted to fertility rites became Easter (but we still retained the ancient fertility symbols such as rabbits).

When the population was small, only a few men and women were able to communicate directly with the super-intelligence, receive prophecies of the future, and undergo mysterious distortions of their own reality. But now that there are over four billion people scratching around on this planet trying to survive, the number of prophets has grown in direct ratio.

Millions are now receiving fragmentary glimpses of the future. Millions are now coming into contact with strange apparitions. The population will almost double in the next 20 years, and we will find ourselves in the midst of many millions of prophets, haunted people, UFO contactees, and bewildered psychics.

This, then, is the first law that governs occult events: such events do not necessarily increase during specific periods of time. Instead, the number of people capable of having these experiences increases, as the population increases.

DARWIN VERSUS VON DÄNIKEN

Earthlings come in a wide variety of distinctive forms. If we had all sprung from a common seed, like a small band of colonists from another planet, we should all be approximately the same in size, color, bone structure, and general racial characteristics.

This is not the case. Anthropologists are still busy cataloging the many differences among the people from different continents. The erect, gangling Homo sapiens appeared suddenly, even mysteriously, in a thousand isolated places around the world somewhere between 70,000 and five million years ago (scientific estimates vary).

We developed slowly according to the conditions of our immediate environment. We were not very smart in the beginning, nor did we have any real culture. If we had come from another world, we would have certainly brought along the culture of that world with us, and we would have been bright enough to build homes and societies from the outset of our visit to Earth.

If early man had been dumped here from somewhere else, or even if this planet was used as a penal colony for misfits (another recurrent theory in ufology), we would not have retrogressed to the caveman stage. We would, in all likelihood, have built shining cities 100,000 years ago, and by now we would be exploring the far reaches of the galaxy with a technology far advanced beyond our present one.

History and folklore tell us that we were still in pretty miserable shape a mere 5,000 years ago. Then, suddenly, we were visited by assorted strangers who taught us agriculture and gave us the first laws, to lead us to a more civilized state. Some of these strangers were said to have come out of the oceans and seas. Others descended from the skies. They were our first gods, and the men who chanced to meet with them and learn from them became our kings, prophets, and priests.

These men underwent peculiar changes after their encounters, and ruled by "divine right" because they were somehow different from the rest of us. Their children inherited their powers – their psychic ability to see and communicate with supernatural beings. For thousands of years, these talents were rare, because the population was small.

But as the population grew and crossbreeding took effect, more and more people inherited these abilities, just as people capable of painting realistic pictures or writing beautiful poetry were once rare, but are now fairly commonplace. The modern cultural "explosion" is related directly to the population explosion. The modern explosion in supernatural experiences is likewise an offshoot of the population explosion.

Who were those gods of yesteryear? Von Däniken assumes they were astronauts. Occultists assume they were elemental demons, mischievous entities that coexist with us beyond the range of our vision – the original serpent people. Scientists have no explanation for them at all, except to dismiss them as "mere mythical figures."

We sat in caves and treetops for a very long time, until this force was introduced and got us moving. First it gave a few men new insights into their surroundings, and helped to mold the social systems that improved our chances for survival. Our own historical records tell us how it then led us into religious wars, led by prophets and visionaries, to further improve and expand those social systems.

Early in the game, it became apparent that two separate forces were at work, and we interpreted this as a war between gods and demons. The gods were von Däniken's mysterious sky people. The demons were the mischievous serpent people. We became so certain and so enthralled with this interpretation that it clouded our vision and confused us for many centuries.

Meanwhile, we were being subtly manipulated toward a distant future goal – a collective destiny that we still cannot fully discern. Even the delicate programming and reprogramming process was hidden from us until the second half of the 20th century. But now the phenomenon is slowly but surely revealing itself to us.

The gods of the ancients are returning, Erich von Däniken tells us. But actually they have been here all along. Through our studies of UFO contacts and contactees, we are beginning to understand what is really going on. While millions of people have been having casual sightings of strange things in the sky and on the ground, other millions have literally been abducted by the phenomenon and subjected to a brainwashing process.

They emerge from the experience with total amnesia, or with a vague, dreamlike memory of what happened. But their lives change suddenly and remarkably. Their intelligence is often sharply increased. Their characters and personalities are altered. In several well-documented cases, their chronic ailments have suddenly been cured. They often divorce their spouses, abandon their families, change their names, and move into new and better jobs.

The process is more sophisticated now than it was in the time of the cavemen, because we are more sophisticated ourselves. We have changed slowly, and improved slowly, over those thousands of years.

In other ages, these experiences were regarded as supernatural and mystical. Today, we try to fit them into a technological framework. We view the contact stories with some alarm, fearing that an alien race is trying to take us over. One group of ufologists is, in fact, convinced that some of these brainwashed humans have managed to attain top jobs in government and industry, and that the affairs of the world are now being controlled by extraterrestrial aliens.

However, the phenomenon does not really seem interested in our mundane day-to-day affairs, except where they may influence their mysterious long-range plan. Darwin was partially right, perhaps, when he speculated about a process of evolution. But he did not see it as a completely controlled process. He lacked the historical perspective needed to view the development of mankind as a series of rungs on a long ladder of enlightenment. The phenomenon was completely hidden from view in his day.

The flaw in the ancient astronaut theory is the absence of motive. They arrived quietly, gave us some guidance, and then went away just as quietly. Were we just the recipients of an exercise in benevolence? Or were they already making plans for us?

If we really are biochemical robots constructed by some mad scientist in ancient times, we were undoubtedly meant to serve some purpose. An Adam and Eve could not fulfill that purpose. The manufacturer needed millions of models to achieve his goal. It has taken a very long time, and required the careful conditioning of billions of people.

Now the nature of that conditioning is slowly being revealed to us, perhaps as a first step toward revealing the entire master plan. The final revelation may not come in our generation, however, or even in the next dozen generations. The phenomenon is in no hurry.

We were first directly controlled by our manufacturers. We called them gods and worshipped them. Before they departed, they set up a system of rule based on "god-kings" – human beings who had been processed and given hereditary powers not possessed by the general population.

The planet was divided up among about 30 of these god-kings, and their system remained in effect for thousands of years, surviving well into the modern industrial age. But the mode of control gradually became diluted and polluted by human greed, politics, and religion. Finally, it collapsed altogether.

The conflict between the serpent people and the rulers of the biochemical robots has continued, however, and the situation is now so desperate that both sides seem willing to expose their modus operandi to us, through overt action in the framework of the UFO phenomenon. In other ages, we accepted this conflict as a battle for men's souls. Now it is becoming apparent that there is more at stake.

We, the biochemical robots, are the prize!

The serpent people – the anti-human forces – are imitating the UFO phenomenon through hallucinations and distortions of reality to confuse us, while the gods are trying to reveal more of themselves and their purpose to us. Millions of people are now able to see beyond the visible spectrum and to sense the presence of these forces. Our two very different worlds are beginning to overlap.

The future will bring a series of small climaxes, explosions of sudden insights and information, and a gradual strengthening of the communication channels between us and "them." As our awareness increases, we may become more and more subservient to these forces, sliding back to our ancient condition – when we were enslaved by them.

The process of change is already underway. The UFO phenomenon is rapidly becoming a new religion. A religion based on the premise that we are inferior to some advanced race from another world – a race that is coming to save us from ourselves.

The basic theme of UFO contact has been anarchism and the promise of a marvelous new socio-religious system. It has almost been an election campaign. The promises have been dazzling, but there has been no attempt to fulfill them. The ancient gods, and their successors, the god-kings, lied to us and manipulated us, and there's no indication that the tactics of the modern ufonauts are any different.

If we are biochemical robots helplessly controlled by forces that can scramble our brains, destroy our memories, and use us in any way they see fit, then we are caught up in a poker game being played with marked cards. Someone seems to be trying to tip us off about the marked deck, but we are like the inveterate gambler who, when informed that the game is crooked, shrugs and says, "But it's the only game in town."

CHAPTER 11

THE ANTIQUITY OF CIVILIZED MAN – M.K. JESSUP – 1958

There is much evidence to show that there have been two "waves" or "surges" of civilization upon Earth, third planet from the sun. Ours is the second "wave," and as such, it is essentially in its infancy, and is the result of slowly reviving embers of a fire, long since quenched, which once covered the world with megalithic stone structures we have not yet learned to emulate.

Those who oppose the idea of a wave of civilization prior to ours, usually do so on dogmatic and categorical grounds. Largely, it seems a matter of our ego and dignity, exemplified more often than not in our religions. Perhaps the arguments pro and con for extreme antiquity have raged around the Atlantis theme more than any other single item.

This is one bone of contention that evokes crusading fervor for both sides. But both sides make a fundamental error that weakens their respective cases. They dissipate their energy debating on where, geographically speaking, Atlantis was located. The pros, very largely, stick to the original tradition, based on Plato, that Atlantis was an island in the Atlantic Ocean. The cons refute this on physical and geological grounds. Both miss the main point, and fan the air uselessly.

If, instead of where, we debate *what* Atlantis was, we can be more rational. It is becoming constantly less debatable that there was, some 8000 to 20,000 years ago, a vast cataclysm on this planet, which produced catastrophic changes on its surface. It has been called: the "Flood"; a collision of worlds; the impact of a comet; a shifting of the globe about its axis of rotation; the movement of polar ice; and so on. For this discussion, the exact nature of it is unimportant.

Something did happen. Something annihilated worldwide civilization, and almost exterminated our race. It could have been a relatively simple occurrence, or a complex of coincident events. I lean toward the thought that a vast meteor swarm, composed of a multitude of miscellaneous debris, struck the earth, probably in what is now the north tropical latitudes of the Western Hemisphere.

There is not room here to develop this theme, but there are many good books to study. One is a privately published book called *Target Earth*, which shows that many geographical features of North and Central America are shaped like vast lunar craters, and appear to have originated from impacts.

But that only tends to prove that there was a cataclysm. It doesn't prove what went before.

There are a number of minor proofs of the antediluvian culture of man. Some are in Charles Fort's books, and some are listed in *The Case for the UFO*; but the one that is most conclusive is the worldwide existence of structures made up of huge stone monoliths or megaliths.

These large pieces of rock are of all sizes up to 8000 tons in weight, and it is not reasonable that so many of them were used by isolated local "civilizations," each building one city and developing independently the means for handling stone. But there is also proof that the builders were of one culture, and this lies in the similar mathematics used, and their manner of grinding these megaliths into place by rubbing in situ.

Further study will be most convincing. Almost without exception, there is indication that work was stopped by unexpected catastrophe, and in some cases antiquity is attested by superimposed glaciation, or by physical disruption due to the rising of mountain chains on which the cities were built.

Archaeological studies break down completely at periods of 1000 to 7000 years, depending on the locality, and often, at those points, the student is confronted with a ready-made civilization or culture, which had to come from somewhere, but whose origin he cannot explain!

If we concede that Atlantis, for example, was but a part of this antiquity, then we gain more by discussing what and when, than by where. Churchward, in *The Lost Continent of Mu*, states the case most logically. He may be wrong in detail, and his geography may be imperfect, but his idea is sound – that there is a common denominator to all of our civilizations of the past 10,000 years. Baalbeck, Egypt, Angkor Wat, Ceylon, Easter Island, Tibet, and Nepal, each speak loudly for an advanced race before the "Flood."

Peru speaks eloquently, for the ruins of Sacsahuaman, Machu Picchu, and Tiahuanaco most certainly predate the Andes, or at least the glaciation which has at one time smoothed off some of the mountaintops; and the vast network of "Nazca lines" on the Peruvian desert was not placed there yesterday by the ignorant race of ground dwellers found by the Spaniards.

There are upwards of 1700 bibliographical references on Atlantis and a few on Mu. But very few are based on fundamentals, and most of them debate merely whether Atlantis was an island in the Atlantic. Perhaps the best general statement for pre-diluvian civilization is Churchward's, but many others are good. The best current book against the antiquity of Man is de Camp's "Lost Continents," and it contains excellent bibliographical references for both sides of the argument.

Leaving aside the details of where Atlantis or Mu might have been located, let us consider: 1) Worldwide similarity of stone works as to size and technique of workmanship, obviously installed before a catastrophe, and before mountains were raised; 2) A block of intelligently worked meteoric steel buried in tertiary coal beds at least 300,000 years ago; 3) A pitcher, or vessel, of strange alloy, inlaid in silver of archaic design, blasted out of solid stone in a quarry in Massachusetts; 4) A gold thread taken from solid stone, 15 feet below the surface, in England; 5) A coin found 120 feet below the surface when drilling a well in Illinois; 6) A slate wall with inscription, in a coal seam in Ohio; and perhaps 7) Records of Egypt, Nepal and Tibet that actually describe some phases of culture, literacy, and mechanical development of 70,000 to 270,000 years ago.

Nothing but the common denominator of worldwide antiquity of Man will solve the problems archaeology has created for itself through a foreshortened time scale.

Here is an extremely interesting "Fortean" item, reprinted in the August 8, 1957 edition of *The Harriman Record* (Tennessee), originally printed in the January 6, 1898 edition of another Harriman newspaper:

> Scientists in Binghamton, New York are puzzled over an aerial visitor that dropped in that vicinity recently. Professor Jeremiah McDonald, who resides on Park Avenue, was returning home at an early hour in the morning when there was a blinding flash of light and an object buried itself in the ground a short distance from his premises.
>
> Later it was dug up and found to be a mass of some foreign substance that had been fused by intense heat. It was still hot, and when cooled off in water was broken open. Inside was found what might have been a piece of metal, in which were a number of curious marks that some think to be characters.

When opened, the stone emitted a strong sulfurous smell. Professor Whitney of the high school declared it an aerolite, but different from anything he had ever seen. The metal had been fused to a whitish substance and it is of unknown quality to the scientific men who have examined it.

CHAPTER 12

THE LEGENDS OF MOUNT SHASTA – RICHARD COHEN – 1980

Many books and stories have been written on the subject of lost civilizations – ancient races whose way of life was, in many ways, superior to ours of today. But to me, the most fascinating of these tales concern ancient civilizations that may still be in existence.

Right here in the United States, the area surrounding Mount Shasta, California has been the cause of a great many legends. The "Mystery People" who are said to have lived there until very recently (and who may still be there), resent intrusion upon their privacy by outsiders, and there are many occasions when they are said to have used their mystical powers to turn visitors away.

There are several stories from the early days of the automobile, stating that when motorists would reach a certain point on the road to Mount Shasta, a light would flash before the startled eyes of the tourists, and the electrical system of their car would cease functioning.

Not until the driver had backed down the road for a hundred feet or more would the engine regain its normal powers. The absence of such occurrences today would seem to indicate that the "residents" of the Shasta forest have either died out or intermingled with the modern inhabitants of the region.

It is also claimed that whenever forest fires have approached close to the forest near Mount Shasta, a strange fog has suddenly emanated from the section occupied by these peculiar people. This fog rises from the ground, in a circular manner, so as to form a wall around the entire region, through which forest fires have never penetrated.

Some natives in this area take delight in taking skeptics on the "circle" tour, pointing out to them the mute evidence: a ring of burnt trees that enclose the mysterious region. Inside of this circle, the trees rise to great heights, are of old age, and are without a single scar or blemish. Outside of the circle, only two hundred feet from the pristine trees, are many battle-scarred veterans of fires.

People living in that part of California also claim that strange cattle, unlike anything ever seen in America, have emerged from the woods. But before going very far along the highways or byways, these animals are frightened by some invisible signal, and abruptly turn around and run back to the place from which they came.

Flying saucers are a part of these legends, too. However, these saucers are not disc-shaped, but elongated like a cigar. In the old days, these "cigars" were called "aerial submarines," because of their resemblance in shape to a sub. Instead of going through the water, these mysterious vessels sailed through the air.

However, they were equally capable of landing on the ocean and acting like a conventional ship. This ability to fly through the air and land on water was not the only accomplishment of these vessels of the "Mystery People," for the "aerial submarines" could *also* function like an ordinary submarine and travel underwater, as well as dive to great depths under the surface.

There are hundreds of people who have testified to seeing these peculiarly shaped boats flown out of the Mount Shasta region, high in the air over the hills and valleys of California. Similar flying "cigars" have been seen by sailors on the high seas, coming and going from remote Pacific islands. These peculiar vessels have been seen as far north as the Aleutian Islands.

In 1951, the following account was written concerning a sighting near Mount Shasta: "Recently, a group of persons playing on one of the golf links of California near the foothills of the Sierra Nevada range, saw a peculiar silver vessel rise in the air, float over the mountaintops, and disappear. It was unlike any airship ever seen. There was absolutely no noise emanating from it, indicating that it was not propelled by a conventional motor."

The theory is that Mount Shasta is inhabited by a race of people who are survivors of the lost continent of Lemuria. Even in modern times, they have continued to manufacture their principal necessities, and have kept themselves carefully isolated from the outside world. One reason these people are not by outsiders is that they have constructed their city within the great mountain itself. Only on rare occasions do they come outside, to hold their various tribal celebrations.

There is said to be a tunnel through the eastern base of Mount Shasta, leading to a city of strange homes. The heat and smoke that can be seen arising from the crater of the mountain comes from this interior city. This is not an unusual tale, inasmuch as there are records indicating that in Mexico, other descendants of the Lemurians are living in an extinct volcano, too – hidden from all possible worldly observation.

Thus, if we are to believe the testimony of many reliable people, we are led to the possibility that a fascinating and totally unknown people lived in California until very recently. Whether these people continue to practice their ancient rites and live as they always did, or whether they have finally adopted modern methods, is an unanswered question. I urge interested parties to visit Mount Shasta and investigate the truth of these stories.

CHAPTER 13

Mr. Dove, who has been a frequent contributor to our magazines over the years, is a well-known amateur astronomer. He believes that the flying saucers come from the planet Mars, and several years ago he drew up a very detailed chart that scientifically correlates sighting "flaps" with the nearness of Mars.

Here, he discusses his theory that certain humanoids seen for the last 200 years may be from Mars. These humanoids sound like an eerie combination of the Spring-Heeled Jack and Mothman. While certain researchers (e.g., Loren Coleman) have tried to confuse the "Grinning Man" with the Spring-Heeled Jack (and both of those with Indrid Cold), there is little in the data to suggest that the Grinning Man even exists. Might we suggest the cryptozoologists give up their attempts to confuse the public about Fortean phenomena, and go back to collecting Bigfoot prints?

HUMANOIDS AND THE MARS SAUCER CYCLE – LONZO DOVE – 1962

In *Fate* magazine for October 1961, there is an article by J. Vyner, reprinted from the British magazine *Flying Saucer Review*, which is a most enlightening collection of reports about the visitations of an unearthly humanoid.

I have taken the trouble to calculate and correlate the dates of these visitations with the periodic flying saucer dates in my established chart of saucer reports, as they recur in the Mars-Earth synodic period of 780 days. They do correspond chronologically with the proper dates for the shortest space journeys between Mars and Earth.

Does this peculiar repeated pattern for these living creatures prove conclusively that they arrive and depart in flying saucers from Mars? Read and decide for yourself.

The strange manlike visitor is described as thin, extremely agile, and wearing a tight metallic-looking suit, metal helmet, and blue-flashing lamp on his chest, which can beam paralyzing rays. This creature was wrapped in a loose, flowing cloak hiding a mysterious bulge on his back, and he was able to leap over high walls.

His ears were pointed, like a member of the cat species. His eyes were round and red, like a bird, and his nose was beaklike. He had flying ability, and hands like a man, but claws like a beast. He tried to contact human beings gently, until fright at his sight caused alarm. He could speak understandable English.

This creature appeared near London in the middle of November 1837, scaring people, until finally a reward was offered for his capture. This date in the Mars-Earth synodic period, set parallel with modern saucer report periods, proves to be a regular saucer appearance date of low intensity, which occurs one or two months after the greater observed "rest" date in the Mars-Earth schedule.

This 1837 sighting occurred one Earth year after the close approach of Mars to Earth, and 13 months after the main short transit time. About a century later, on June 18th, 1953, a similar creature was sighted, with wings showing on his back, at Houston, Texas. This date was also 13 months after the close approach of Mars to Earth.

The *Fate* article lacks the detail that at 2:30 a.m. on the date of the above-mentioned Houston sighting, Hilda Walker and two other witnesses saw the "winged man," and after he was gone, an *oval object flew over the house.* Then, two days later, the well-known Brush Creek landing occurred, in which little men were seen dipping water outside their flying saucer. This was seven days after many people saw flying discs in California, New Mexico, Connecticut, and Belgium, between June 13th and 14th, 1953.

A century earlier, on February 18th and 20th, 1838 – also 13 months after the Mars close-approach to Earth of that period – the same creature reappeared in English villages three months after the visits already described. A lady answered her doorbell and invited the "beast" in – until the lights revealed his face and figure, and she screamed in alarm.

Seven days later, the space visitor again sought in vain for human reception, when he asked in the English language to be escorted to Mr. Ashworth of Commercial Road in England. The butler was terrified, and slammed the door.

Another sighting occurred about four months later, on the night of July 6th, 1838 – a date exactly analogous to the periodic "saucer landing" times in my chart, which is about two months before the proper astronautic time for return from planet Earth to Mars. This would be the best time for "exploration" on Earth.

At Liverpool, England, a police inspector named Hemer turned his back when he saw a flash in the sky, and a great round fiery object landed in a field. This date, by the way, is precisely analogous to the famous Kenneth Arnold flying saucer activity peak of June-July 1947. (The next analogical period, August 1949, was the time of the hushed Death Valley saucer landing in which "little people" were seen.)

The creature was back again on October 3rd, 1883 at Warwick, England, at signal time for new launchings of saucers from Mars to Earth. About three years earlier, on July 28th, 1880, right on the usual "rest" date after an 11-month (or half-Mars year) of saucer activity – a date always marked by spectacular events – a humanoid creature of similar description was seen at Louisville, Kentucky.

The *Fate* article does not mention that on the same date, between 6 and 7 p.m., there appeared a "double globe" and a separate satellite disk moving up and down in the sky at Louisville and Madisonville in Kentucky. Nor does *Fate* mention that this Louisville landing occurred four months after luminous disks orbited, east to west, over Kettenau in Germany, on March 22nd, 1880 – the proper and observed saucer arrival time, via the "long, easy spiral route," from Mars to Earth.

According to the *Fate* article, the creature was seen again on January 6th, 1948 at Chehalis in Washington State. Somehow this item failed to come into my vast file of saucer reports, probably because "monster" cases were not yet being connected with flying saucers.

But I observe that the date was just one day before the tragic case of Captain Mantell, whose plane was shattered out of the skies while chasing a huge flying saucer near Fort Knox, Kentucky on January 7th, 1948. This was about one month before the close approach of Mars to Earth on February 17th – exactly two Mars-Earth periods before the great saucer peak of April 15-17, 1952.

Again on the analogous "rest" date, in late August 1944, the creature appeared at Mattoon in Illinois, looking through windows and stunning people with his ray lamp. He escaped the dragnet of policemen sent to get him.

My files show that three months later, the "foo fighter" fireballs began to chase American war planes on November 23rd, 1944. This again is about a month before the usual saucer activity time, 13 months after the Mars approach to Earth, like the above case of June 1952.

About 2,500 years ago, the same species of living creature, in the same kind of flying "bowl," landed in front of the Temple of Jerusalem, built by Solomon 400 years earlier. The form of this "saucer" ("Gilgal" in Hebrew) was commemorated on the first Hebrew coins ever minted, by King Simon Maccabeus in 141 B.C., preserved to our day in archaeological ruins. The following is quoted from the first chapter of Ezekiel:

As for the likeness of the living creatures, they had the likeness of a man, had four wings, their feet were straight, the sole of their feet was like the sole of a calf's foot, and they sparkled like burnished brass; they had hands of a man, they had the face of a man, of a lion, of an ox, also the face of an eagle.

They went straight forward, they turned not when they went, and ran and returned as a flash of lightning. The appearance of torches (flash-lamps) went up and down among the living creatures, and the fire was bright, and out of the fire went forth lightning (flash-beams). As for the wheels, they were called in my hearing "the Gilgal."

On May 31st, 1960, at 7:50 to 7:57 p.m., in Washington, D.C., I had a good long look at the real thing, as it descended slowly in the sky, lighting it up like a star. The same object was observed a few evenings later by a scientist at the university where I was then employed as an astro-technician. This occurred between the "saucer landing" and "return to Mars" dates on my chart.

I do feel it is manifestly possible that the humanoid living creatures reported during certain saucer sighting peaks are passengers from Mars in flying saucers.

CHAPTER 14

For more than twenty years, the world has watched UFOs haunting our skies, and marveled at the tales of spacemen landing on Earth. Still, the mystery remains unsolved. Thrilling expectancy has fallen to frustration; hopes of Messiahs regenerating our lost humanity are fading to disillusion.

Religion, philosophy, politics, science, art – all have failed to give mankind the inspiration we need. In our secret souls, we realize salvation must come from the stars.

In their impatience, people believe the spacemen to be new arrivals, come to mock the follies of men. They cannot conceive that the celestials have been surveilling our Earth since civilization began. Ancient records, from every country in the world, all agree that long ago, our Earth gloried in a golden age, ruled by divine dynasties, teaching the wisdom of the planets. But men rebelled. War was waged with fantastic weapons, followed by cataclysms plunging mankind to barbarism.

Slowly, man climbed again to civilization, inspired by solitary teachers from space. Garbled folkloric memories imagined these celestials as Gods, worshipped under different names by all the peoples of antiquity.

Such novel interpretation of the past bewilders our minds conditioned to the present conventional views of evolution. Proof that Earth was once ruled by spacemen who inspired our civilization would surely be the most fundamental discovery of the 20th century.

Acceptance of the evidence proving celestial intervention in terrestrial affairs would revolutionize our geocentric ideas, and inspire men to cosmic consciousness, ascending to harmony of soul with our brothers from space. Astronomers have recanted their former nihilism and now teach that our Earth is but one of billions of inhabited planets, many with civilizations transcending our own.

No longer dare we believe that the same God sustaining this wondrous universe with that parallel universe of antimatter (and those myriad astral and ethereal realms) would show special favor to our tiny Earth and somehow enter His vast creation to live among men on this grain of dust. The "gods" who did manifest in antiquity were beings with wisdom, emotion, and passion. They dominated mankind in a grandiose age of wonder. They were spacemen.

Students of UFOs divining the tremendous revolution in thought the spacemen reveal often feel like the little boy in Hans Christian Anderson's wonderful tale, *The Emperor's New Clothes*, who, while his dutiful elders admired the suit of gold, tried to protest that the monarch was ambling around in the nude.

Our Western culture was originally evolved from the teachings of Greece and Israel, and expanded by the enquiries of science since the 17th century. This basic knowledge determines our thought patterns today. The Greek philosophers and the Christian fathers were no doubt learned and pious men, fully conversant with the doctrines of their own times. They were apparently unaware of those wonderful civilizations of the ancient east, with their millennial-long experience and ageless wisdom.

Darwin and Einstein, whose theories still shape modern science, were most brilliant and inspired intellects. However, they took no cognizance of UFO phenomena. Today, men of genius delve with insight into special research, but outside their particular field, they are usually ignorant of other subjects and accept conventional views often decades out of date. Many of our fundamental conceptions are based on false premises. It seems that no single mind can synthesize the glorious panorama presented by our new knowledge.

Cogent examples could be quoted showing how even the experts wildly disagree when evaluating identical phenomena. It should suffice to contrast three different interpretations of flying crosses, which are actually a matter of profound importance.

In the early hours of Tuesday morning, October 24th, 1967 near Okehampton, Devon, England, police constables Roger Willey and Clifford Waycott were astonished to see, in the night sky, a very large and bright object in the shape of a cross, which they followed for about twelve miles. Then, it suddenly disappeared.

Similar crosses were seen later by reputable observers in many parts of England. Though evidence from these worthy police officers against any offending motorist would have been readily accepted in any court of law, on this occasion, their testimony was doubted, for officials from the Ministry of Defense insisted that the constables must have seen an American aircraft refueling at night (although the U.S. Air Force in Britain reported that no such operation took place in England during that period stated).

Suppose, against our better judgment, we accept the Ministry's explanation. We thank their official expert for his enlightenment, and then comment that in A.D. 1189, William of Newbury, the mediaeval chronicler, reports in *Historia Anglicana*:

> In the terrible silence, a surpassing and greatly astonishing
> prodigy was seen about this time, in England, by many who
> up to the present time bear witness to those who did not see it.
> Above the public road which continued to London, a village
> by no means wretched, called Dunstaple, by chance, so to
> speak, an hour after noon, those who looked up at the sky saw,
> in the serene vault of heaven, the striking shape of the emblem
> of our Lord, with a dazzling milk-white whiteness and the
> conjoined form of a man crucified, which is painted in church
> to the memory of the passion of Our Lord and the devotion of
> the faithful.

Thirty-eight years later, in A.D. 1227, in similar curious Latin, the scholar
Matthew of Paris reports in *Historia Anglorum*:

> At the same time in Germany, while Master Oliver was
> preaching (for the Crusades), there appeared manifest to all
> the people a crucifix in the air, on account of which sealed
> letters were sent by several churchmen to the University of
> Paris, and they were read out to the public.

Eager for truth, we ask casually, "Would those crosses be American airplanes
refueling?"

"Yes, quite!" agrees our expert. Suddenly, he frowns and asks, "When was
it? 1200? Oh, the Americans were not civilized in those days; they had no
airplanes, only bows and arrows. Those people in the middle ages must have
seen the planet Venus."

There is nothing like asking someone who really knows! We gratefully
acknowledge the expert's explanation, then, as an afterthought, we
remember the fourth-century bishop, Eusebius, describing Constantine's
conversion to Christianity, as told to him by the emperor himself. From his
Life of Constantine, Book 1, Chapter 28, we quote for the year A.D. 312,
possibly in the Alps:

> He called upon this God therefore in his prayers, entreating
> and beseeching him that, wherever he was, he would manifest
> himself to him and reach out his right hand (to his assistance)
> in his present affairs. Whilst the emperor was putting up those
> prayers and earnest supplications, a most wonderful sign from
> God appeared, which (sign) had any other person given a
> relation of it would not easily have been received as true.

But since the victorious emperor himself told it to us who write this history, a long while after, namely at such time as we were vouchsafed his knowledge and converse and confirmed his relation with an oath, who will hereafter doubt of giving credit to his narrative. Especially when the succeeding times gave an evident attestation to this relation.

About the meridian hours of the sun, when the day was declining, he said he saw with his own eyes the trophy of the cross in the heavens, placed over the sun made up of light, on an inscription annexed to it containing the words "BY THIS I CONQUER." And that at the sight thereof, an amazement seized both him and all his military forces, which followed him as he was making a journey some whither, and were spectator of the miracle.

This luminous cross with its skywriting at once prompted Constantine to enlist the aid of the Christians; he soon defeated and killed Emperor Maxentius, and in gratitude, established Christianity as the state religion of Rome. Since he later had his wife, son, and nephew put to death, Constantine's conversion was hardly complete.

We ask our official expert whether the cross was a Roman airplane or just the planet Venus. Somewhat baffled, he admits, "I don't think the Romans had airplanes. Constantine and his army must have seen Venus." He adds hastily, "Christians? I think there is something odd about this sighting. You should ask the archbishop of Canterbury!"

We then wander round to Lambeth Palace, knock on the great door, and seek audience with His Grace. We tell the archbishop about those fiery crosses seen by the police officers in 1967 interpreted as airplanes, the crosses in the middle ages said to be Venus, and ask him about the famous cross seen by Constantine and all his soldiers in A.D. 312.

His Grace smiles benignly, and explains that the cross was a sign sent by God to inspire Constantine to turn Christian. Without that cross, Constantine would probably have been defeated and killed, the Christians persecuted, and to this very day, Rome would have worshipped pagan gods. That cross in the sky in A.D. 312 was instrumental in establishing Christianity.

We would then agree, and venture to point out that the cross seen by everyone must have been a spaceship, the alleged skywriting some phenomena of its forcefield. Christendom founded by spacemen! The archbishop admonishes us for blasphemy, and asks us to leave.

Fiery crosses in 1967, 1227, 1189, and 312 – American airplanes refueling in the sky, the planet Venus, a sign from God! Millions of people fervently believe these explanations. Our simple souls cannot cope with such subtleties. To us, all those fiery crosses were simply spaceships surveilling Earth.

People who have marveled at the UFOs during the last two decades are astonished to learn that the sightings witnessed today can be paralleled by similar phenomena centuries ago. On June 24th, 1947 near Mt. Rainier in Washington, Kenneth Arnold saw nine flying saucers heralding our age of UFOs; in the year 9 B.C., the Japanese saw the skies of their cherry-blossom island haunted by nine sun disks.

On November 20th, 1952, George Adamski met Orthon from Venus in the California desert, an encounter still discussed; the *Nihongi*, chronicles of Old Japan, vividly describe how, in A.D. 460, the emperor went hunting with bow and arrows on Mt. Katsuraki, when suddenly, a tall noble stranger appeared, who said he was a "god assuming mortal form." The pair honored each other with courtesies, and spent the day hunting deer together, matching hit for hit.

On February 18th, 1953, Adamski claims to have gone for a trip in a spaceship where he conversed with a Venusian master; in the sixth century B.C., the Greek poet, Aethalides, rhapsodized over his travels to Hades and to realms above the earth.

In 1952, Truman Bethurum described how he met the beautiful Aura Rhanes, captain of a spaceship from the unknown planet, Clarion. She alleged that spacemen and spacewomen indistinguishable from ourselves are living among us. Livy and Dionysius of Halicarnassus tell wonderful tales of the early Roman king, Numa Pompilius, who about 700 B.C., married the nymph, Egeria, who taught him much cosmic wisdom.

Those humanoids plaguing South America resemble the satyrs of Greece. In 490 B.C., Darius, king of Persia, invaded Greece. The Athenians sought aid from Sparta. Herodotus describes how the runner, Philippides, met the god, Pan, on Mt. Parthenium, who promised divine aid.

During the battle of Marathon, the victorious Athenians swore that several gods fought in their foremost ranks, just as eight years earlier, Castor and Pollux were believed to have fought for Rome to win the battle against the Tusculans at Lake Regillus.

After their great victory, the Athenians raised a temple to Pan. Zeus, Apollo and those cavalier gods winging down to Greece, for amorous exploits, were surely handsome spacemen. What powerful motive made the Greeks, lovers of classical beauty, worship Pan, a grotesque humanoid?

On November 4th, 1957 a dazzling UFO plunged down from the night sky to hover over the Brazilian fort of Itaipu; as two sentries stared in alarm, they were suddenly scorched by powerful heat rays, which also cut out electrical circuits and convulsed the garrison to panic.

The people of Britain were startled on July 16th, 1963 by a mysterious crater, eight feet in diameter, which suddenly appeared overnight in a barley and potato field at Manor farm, Charlton, Wiltshire. A patch of earth was completely denuded of potatoes, evoking rumors of a landing of a spaceship from Uranus.

The authorities hurriedly attributed the hole to a meteorite, which could not be found. Similar craters have occurred in many countries, often coincident with the sightings of UFOs. It is generally believed that such craters may be caused by pressure from the gravitational forcefield of spaceships, which depresses the ground and removes the crops.

Julius Obsequens, the fourth-century Roman writer who collected accounts of strange phenomena like Charles Fort, reported in 82 B.C.: "During the era of Sulla, a great clash of standards and arms, with dreadful shouting, was heard between Capua and Volturnum, so that two armies seemed to be locked in combat for several days. When men investigated this marvel more closely, the tracks of horses and of men and freshly trampled grass and shrubs seemed to foretell the burden of a huge war."

Might this devastation – *where there had been no fighting* – suggest the landing of a spaceship?

Those rains of flesh and blood falling from the sky, mentioned by Charles Fort and reporters today, are now construed as evidence of spaceships. On takeoff, the ship's magnetic forcefield may carry away animals, birds, even humans, which are later jettisoned from a great height.

In the sixteenth century, the young Alsatian priest, Conrad Wolffhart, fascinated by erratic phenomena, scoured the classics for bizarre facts and supplemented the data quoted by Julius Obsequens, many of whose writings were lost.

Wolffhart hellenized his name to Lycosthenes and chronicled strange sightings in earth, sea, and sky from ancient times up to 1556. *Prodigiorum Libellus* by Lycosthenes and Obsequens, published in Latin by Samuel Luchmanns in Lyons in 1720, records that about 461 B.C., in the consulships of P. Volumnius Amentinus and Servius Sulpicius Camerinus:

The ground shook with a mighty earthquake. An ox spoke.

The heavens were seen to glow again. Various apparitions were observed with voices dreadful to the eyes and ears of men. It rained flesh like the appearance of snow from the sky, scattered in pieces large and small, as though torn from every kind of bird flying over before it touched the ground.

The remains, which truly occurred, spread over city and field and lay for a long time, neither changed in color nor smell from old decayed meat. This outrage the soothsayers were unable to interpret. However, the Sibylline Books advised that it warned of enemies without and sedition within the city.

This prodigy was reported by Pliny in his *Historia Naturalis*, Volume 2. During the 5th century B.C., the young republic of Rome was fighting for its life, surrounded by bitter enemies, Etruscans, Samnites and Volscians. It is likely that their conflicts would attract the attention of the spacemen, who were visiting Greece and Israel. After visiting the prophets in Israel, the "Lord" would probably fly over Italy to survey the struggles of Rome.

Rome was founded in 753 B.C. by Romulus, son of the vestal virgin, Rhea Silvia (father: Mars, a celestial). Romulus was transported to the skies, in a cloud, in 716 B.C., while giving judgment on the Palatine hill, witnessed by hundreds of people.

A few days later, Julius Proculus, a Roman senator, swore the most solemn oath that he had met Romulus transfigured, returned from the dead, on the road to Rome. This virgin birth and resurrection of Romulus occurred seven hundred years before Jesus Christ.

The Romans believed Romulus, son of a god, to have returned from the dead in 716 B.C. Christians believe Jesus Christ, Son of God, returned from the dead in 29 B.C. Can we accept one without the other?

Those flying saucers seen today throw wondrous illumination on the past. Perhaps our conventional ideas of evolution and history are wrong? Man stands on the threshold of a new, glorious cosmic age. All our basic beliefs must be reexamined, the truth treasured, the false rejected. If we study again those classics from antiquity in the light of our new knowledge, we shall thrill at the inspiring realization of our heritage from the stars.

SPACE KINGS OF ANCIENT ROME

"The voices of the Fauns have often been heard, and Deities have appeared in forms so visible that they have compelled everyone who is not senseless or hardened in impiety to confess the presence of the Gods."

In his profound study, *De Natura Deorum*, Marcus Tullius expressed the conviction of all Romans that the Gods really did exist in celestial realms, ever ready to influence the affairs of men. The Romans watched the skies for a thousand years, like all the peoples of antiquity worldwide; from the portents, their augurs prophesied the future, proving the deep impression the heavens exerted on everyone's mind.

In *De Divinatione*, Cicero recorded prodigies similar to our own UFO sightings today: "But I return to the divination of the Romans. How often has our Senate enjoined the decimvirs to consult the Books of the Sibyll! For instance, when two suns had been seen, or when three moons had appeared, and when flames of fire were noticed in the night, and the heaven itself seemed to burst open, and strange globes were remarked in it!"

Today, when luminous objects are seen in the sky, our own governments – even in our "Space Age" – dismiss them all as hallucinations, fireballs, or the planet Venus. What flaming memories made the ancients watch such UFOs with alarm? The Romans believed their Eternal City basked under the divine protection of the Gods; its foundation was attended by supernatural powers.

In the 9th century, the Latin city of Alba Longa was ruled by Tiberinus (descended from Aeneas). He lost his life by drowning in a river called Albula, which was renamed Tiber, on which Rome was destined to stand. His son, Amulius, versed in the secret lore of the Etruscans, dabbled with electricity using techniques alien to us. Dio Cassius states:

> Amulius, a descendant of Tiberinus, displayed an overweening pride and dared to make himself a God. He went so far as to match the thunder with artificial thunder, to answer lightning with lightning, and to hurl thunderbolts. He met his end by the sudden overflow of the lake beside which his palace was built; it submerged both him and his palace.

This astounding revelation suggests that around 850 B.C., initiates in old Italy utilized forces verging on atomic fusion! Such a claim evokes our ridicule, yet dispassionate reflection recalls Celestials with annihilating weapons mentioned in the *Mahabharata*, and the fantastic wars that blasted ancient China.

Moses probably learned much of his magic from Jehovah. Amulius no doubt attempted to copy the wonders of visiting spacemen, just as our own scientists are striving to do today. Amulius was not the first man, nor the last, to tamper with some cosmic force and in ignorance, destroy himself.

Later, Alba Longa was ruled by Numitor jointly with his brother, another

Amulius. The latter wrested the kingdom from Numitor and fearing his niece, Rhea Silvia, might have children, he made her Priestess of Vesta, sworn to remain a virgin all her days. Soon afterwards, Rhea Silvia found herself with child, fathered, she alleged, by the God Mars. She became duly delivered of two boys in size and beauty more than human, suggesting divine parentage.

Amulius ordered the twins to be put into a basket and thrown into the Tiber. They drifted downstream and were washed ashore, where they were found and suckled by a "shewolf." The Latin *lupa* also meant prostitute; the "shewolf" probably referred to Larentia, wife of the shepherd, Faustulus, who adopted the infants.

On attaining manhood, Romulus and Remus killed Amulius and decided to build a new city. They agreed to settle their argument, as to the precise place, by divination from the flight of birds. Remus first saw six vultures, then Romulus saw twelve, although some people alleged he had cheated. In their quarrel, Remus was killed. On April 21ˢᵗ, 753 B.C., Romulus founded Rome.

Romulus championed the cause of the people against the grasping patricians; beloved by the soldiers, he became greatly honored. In 716 B.C., while Romulus was delivering judgment on the Palatine Hill, thunder and lightning rent the skies. A black cloud blotted out the sun. When the storm ceased, the assembly were astonished to discover that Romulus had vanished from their midst, miraculously transported to the skies.

Shortly afterwards, Julius Proculus, a man of noblest birth, swore by the most sacred emblems before all the people that he had seen Romulus suddenly descend from the sky and appear to him radiantly transfigured in bright and shining armor. The hero told Proculus that it was the pleasure of the Gods that after founding a city destined to be the greatest on Earth, he should dwell in heaven. The Romans all fervently believed this miracle, and honored Romulus as their God, Quirinus.

Apollodorus mentions that Hercules was translated to the skies in a cloud. Galenus records that Asclepius was raised by angels in a column of fire, as happened also to Dionysius, Ascanius, Enoch, and Elijah. So many heroes transported to the skies. Could the ancients have seen this actually happen?

Born to a virgin. Fathered by a God. Guided by divine omens. Translated to heaven. Seeming resurrection to inspire his followers. Worshipped for centuries as a God. Does this story of Romulus not startle us by its similarity to the wonder of another savior 700 years later?

The Jews believe that Elijah was whisked to heaven in a whirlwind, but scorn the tale of Romulus – only a few hundred miles away and at about the same time – being transported to the skies in a cloud. The dispassionate seeker for truth finds it odd that throughout the centuries, it apparently never occurred to the Jews and Romans that perhaps Jehovah and Jupiter were one-and-the-same God.

The prodigies in Italy surely parallel the marvels of Old Testament Israel. Christians condemn the virgin birth of Romulus, and his miraculous translation and resurrection, as blasphemy, yet revere the very same supernatural attributes accorded to Jesus as divine Truth.

On the evening of August 19, 1962, two glowing red spheres, the size of footballs, were seen hovering over Duas Pontes near Diamantina, Minas Gerais, Brazil. During the night, strange humanoids only 18 inches tall entered the hut of Rivalino Maffra da Silva, a poor diamond prospector, and surveyed the family in bed.

Soon after dawn, his twelve-year-old son found two odd balls on the ground outside, each with a tail and spike. The father came out to look at them. Suddenly, the balls joined together and enveloped him in a cloud of yellow smoke. Sanhor Maffra da Silva vanished. The affair remains a mystery.

Romulus, too, vanished in a cloud. Numa Pompilius was born on the very day that Rome was founded by Romulus. He lived in Cures, an important town of the Sabines. Unusual in that age of barbarism, this young man studied self-discipline and wisdom, devoting his leisure to contemplation serving the Gods.

For a whole year after the disappearance of Romulus, the various factions could not agree on any Roman as King. Eventually, with one accord, they offered the throne to this shy philosopher now nearly forty. Only when finally convinced by the divine omen of a flight of birds over his veiled head did he accept.

This gentle king reorganized the worship of Jupiter, divided the year into twelve months, and ruled in almost continuous peace. But even the greatest philosophers look foolish attempting the impossible. Numa, exasperated by the frivolity of the fair sex, directed that women should be seen but not heard; neither must they meddle or gossip.

After his failure to silence women, Numa turned to the easier task of controlling lightning, where he met with success. The ancients apparently inherited a psychoscience from some advanced civilization and utilized natural electricity, soundwaves, and possibly antigravity – techniques lost to us. The Ark of the Israelites appears to have been a highly charged battery.

The great temples of antiquity were protected by lightning conductors, as initiates called down fire from heaven. Numa anticipated Benjamin Franklin in his experiments with lightning. His discoveries must have been spectacular, for Tullus Hostilius tried to repeat them. Like Amulius a century earlier, Hostilius must have used the wrong formula, for a thunderbolt consumed him and his house.

The few records extant from the 7th century B.C. suggest that extra-terrestrials were particularly active on Earth. In 670 B.C., the "angel of the Lord" annihilated the army of Sennaeherib. In 660 B.C., heavenly deities assisted the Japanese Emperor, Jimmu, against the Ainu. About 630 B.C., Zoroaster beheld God amid fire, probably the radiance of a spaceship on Mount Sabalan. A few decades later, near Babylon, Ezekiel beheld his famous Wheel.

Dionysius of Halicarnassus apparently confirms this outer space activity. Writing of early Rome, he makes a cryptic reference: "Higher up in the clouds, two great armies marching." The hosts of Heaven in Hebrew theology are generally imagined as spiritual angels of light contending against demonic forces of darkness, but even this esoteric vision is probably based on some actual conflict seen in the skies.

It is relevant to note that the Second Book of Maccabees, Chapter V, records "Horsemen running in the air" over Israel in 170 B.C. A similar spectacle before the fall of Jerusalem, in A.D. 70, was reported by Josephus. Matthew of Raris gives a vivid description of two occasions in A.D. 1236, when there appeared in the skies over England and Ireland "armed soldiers superbly although hostilely equipped." Pliny states explicitly:

> We are told that during the wars with the Cimbri (North Germany, 113-101 B.C.), a noise of clanging armor and the sounding of trumpets was heard from the sky, and that the same thing has happened frequently, both before then and later. In the consulship (103 B.C.) of Marius, the inhabitants of Ameria and Tuder (now Todi) saw the spectacle of heavenly armies advancing from the east and west to meet in battle, those from the west being routed.

Many centuries earlier, the *Ramayana* and *Mahabharata* brilliantly described celestial wars in the air above old India. The Etruscans and their contemporaries all over the earth anxiously watched the skies. There must have been some overwhelming cause for their concern. Dare we emulate our science fiction writers and speculate on the fantasy of rival space fleets pursuing their battle in the skies of Earth? Our critics, who were not there to see them, would no doubt raise objections more bizarre than the spectacle suggested.

In 708 B.C., when Rome was ravaged by plague, an *ancile* or bronze shield is said to have fallen from heaven. Numa promptly inspired the suffering people, declaring that the Muses (extraterrestrials?) had told him the marvel was sent by the Gods, an omen signifying their protection of the City. To lessen the chances of theft, the King ordered his most expert craftsman to fashion eleven exact replicas. These "ancilia" were entrusted to the Salii, Priests of Mars, who carried them in religious processions.

The strange metal object from the skies was obviously manufactured and therefore not a meteorite. It cannot have come from outer space, since it would have melted entering the atmosphere. The thing must have fallen from a low height, otherwise its shape would have been greatly distorted upon hitting the ground.

Superstitious though the Romans were, such a highly practical and militant people would hardly worship an ordinary, standard equipment shield, any more than we would accept an oilcan as from a UFO if we could buy a similar one at Woolworth's. Moreover, the Romans must have firmly believed that the Gods actually were flying at that time in their sky, and could drop something on the city.

Plutarch explains that the buckler was not round, nor completely oval, but had a curving indentation, the arms of which were bent back and united with each other at top and bottom. Not knowing what it was, the Romans called the thing a "shield," which it partly resembled.

Bronze plates do not fall from the sky unless someone drops them. The Romans never doubted the ancile's celestial origin, therefore they must have been fully conditioned to acknowledge supermen flying over their city in solid aircraft, just as five hundred years later, in 214 B.C., the citizens of Hadria were astonished to see, in the sky, "an altar around which grouped the forms of men in white garments."

Today, some wild tribe in the Amazon jungle may be dancing around their latest idol, an empty soup can flung from some Brazilian airplane. The Romans venerated the "shield" as sent by the Gods. Surely the thing must have been dropped from a spaceship?

Numa Pompilius sought inspiration in a grove of the Gods watered by a perennial spring, where he could meditate in solitude, free from the clamor of Rome. The King claimed to have been honored with a celestial marriage to the Goddess Egeria, who loved him in a blessed communion that endowed him with wisdom. The Romans stood in awe of Numa's power. They accepted his strange revelations and believed nothing too incredible or impossible.

By the counsel of Egeria, Numa surprised the Gods Picus and Faunus, in their retreat under the Aventine Hill, and kept them prisoners, until Jupiter appeared in the form of lightning and promised his favors, later confirmed by the famous "ancile" dropping from Heaven. Is it too fantastic to wonder if Numa had somehow arrested two spacemen, probably with drugged wine, who were subsequently rescued by a spaceship?

This delightful marriage of Numa and Egeria recalls the *Sataphatha Brahmana* telling of the Apsara, Urvasi, who winged down to marry Pururavas. The medieval chronicle *De Nugis Curialium* describes how, in A.D. 1070, the Saxon patriot, Edrie the Wild, fell in love with a beautiful damsel from space. In 1952, Truman Bethurum claimed to have met Aura Rhanes, a spacewoman from Clarion, who enlightened him on cosmic mysteries. Can we be really sure that our own wives are of this world?

When Numa died tranquilly in 672 B.C., he directed that his twelve books on natural philosophy should be buried in one stone coffin, and himself in another. About four hundred years later, heavy rains washed away the earth disclosing the coffins. The Senate decided that publication of Numa's writings would reveal the most sacred mysteries of the Gods and the state religion, so they ordered all the books to be burned.

Numa's own coffin was found empty! Was Numa resurrected or "translated" by his space wife, Egeria?

In the reign of Numa's successor, Tullus Hostilius, a mighty voice was heard issuing from the grove on the mountaintop, which commanded the people to return to the Gods of their fathers, recalling the Voice of the Lord admonishing Abraham and Moses. In 640 B.C., Tullus was destroyed by fire called down from heaven, as 200 years earlier, the "Angel of the Lord" destroyed those followers of Baal plaguing Elijah.

During the reigns of the succeeding Kings, Ancus Martius, Lucius Tarquinius, and Servius Tullius, Rome was haunted by strange portents perplexing the soothsayers. One day while Tarquinius and his gifted wife, Tanaquil, were at table, a noble slavewoman, Ocresia, was placing food on burning logs when a phallus sprang to her from the flames; Tanaquil interpreted the prodigy as presaging an extraordinary birth.

The King ordered Ocresia to dress in bridal garments. Seated in the heat of the fires, she conceived a son, Servius Tullius, noted for his flame-colored hair – an unlikely tale, yet paralleled by later claims of the conception of illustrious personages fathered by the Holy Ghost, sylphs, or spacemen.

The tyranny of Tarquin, the last King of Rome, goaded the Romans to revolt. In 510 B.C., his son, Sextus, ravished his cousin's wife. This rape of the noble Lucretia outraged the citizens. They deposed Tarquin and established the long Republic of Rome. Tarquin was supported by Lars Porsena of Clusium, who like all Etruscan priest-kings, had studied that strange electrical science still unknown to us.

In a most significant revelation, Pliny recalls that Lars Porsena prayed to the Gods, who hurled thunderbolts to destroy Bolsena, the wealthiest town in Tuscany. Spacemen are not always benevolent. The Sanskrit and Chinese classics gave vivid descriptions of assault from space. The Bible tells how "angels of the Lord" destroyed Sodom and Gomorrah. We can picture a UFO hovering over the Italian town, blitzing it with heat rays, leaving Bolsena in flames, just as in 640 B.C., celestial fire had blasted Tullus Hostilius to death in his own palace. Fantasy? Pliny believed it!

Cicero, in *De Natura Deorum* Book 1, Chapter 2, recorded the firm belief that when Tarquin's ally, Octavius Mamilius, confronted the Romans at Lake Regillus, the dictator, Aulus Posthumus, sought aid from the Gods. Two strange horsemen "beyond the stature of man" appeared, and led the Romans to victory. Aulus Posthumus swore they were the Gods Castor and Pollux, so he erected a temple in their honor.

This magic land of Old Italy seduces our soul. Those mysterious Etruscans; King Amulius submerged by his own explosions; God-begotten Romulus translated to the skies, then resurrected; wise old Numa married to a Nymph, playing with lightning; a shield dropping from heaven; Tullus Hostilius destroyed by a thunderbolt; Servius Tullius conceived by fire; Lars Porsena calling down lightning to burn Bolsena; Castor and Pollux fighting for Rome at Lake Regillus; mysterious voices presaging centuries of strange lights in the sky; apparitions descending among men.

Suddenly, we feel we are reading the Bible. Why must we worship such prodigies in Old Palestine as manifestations of the "Lord," yet ignore identical wonders, at the same time in Italy, not far away?

Should we not write a Second Old Testament about Ancient Rome, inspired by spacemen?

SPACEMEN IN ANCIENT GREECE

The earliest Greeks, like primitive peoples all over the world in far antiquity, worshipped the spacemen as Sky Gods, descending as divine kings to teach the arts and crafts of civilization to aspiring humanity. The Celestials mastered a wondrous science. Some Gods were believed to control thunder, lightning, winds, storms, seas, and the potent, ever-present forces of nature.

Temples were erected on hills as dwelling places of the gods – race memories, perhaps, of the secluded abodes of the space kings in ancient days. Visitants from space or ethereal realms may have occasionally appeared in these sacred retreats, to their initiates, just as in Israel, the "Lord" materialized to his priests within the tabernacle that was taboo to the people. Veneration of the Celestials in Greece, as in China and Japan, developed into the deification of heroes, and then into ancestor worship.

In ancient times, the Gods were not associated with morality. The cavalier zest of lusty Zeus, and his amorous wives and daughters frolicking with their loves on Mount Olympus amused the admiring Greeks, but even the most devoted sycophants could hardly extol the virtues of those playboys in the skies.

Plato, the wisest of the Greeks, in his Laws, solemnly reminded the cynical younger generation, "No one who has adopted in youth that the gods do not exist, ever continued to hold it until he was old."

UFO literature today abounds in well-documented evidence of the landings of nonhumans in isolated places, particularly in South America. Notable experts appear gravely concerned at the invasion. Descriptions of these humanoids, often exuding unpleasant odor, at once recall those fantastic tales of devils reeking of sulfur, alleged to have consorted with witches in the Middle Ages; some correspond uncomfortably with apparitions reported by credible witnesses all over the world.

Similar humanoids appeared in ancient Greece and were worshipped as gods. Greek country folk delighted in the noisy, merry god, Pan, usually represented as a sensual being with horns, a puck nose, and goat's feet. He loved the wild mountains and forests of Arcady, where he frolicked with the woodland nymphs. Sometimes travelers were scared by strange sounds in the wilderness, which they attributed to Pan; their fear coined our word "panic."

Pan was a wonderful musician and son of Hermes (Mercury), a space god. A tortuous, though valid, argument can be advanced to suggest that Pan was a generic term for humanoids similar to those bizarre spacemen now plaguing the peasants of Brazil. Pan's association with music in wild country may have been some poetical connotation for strident noises from spaceships. An admittedly extravagant deduction, yet not wholly untenable as the famous sighting of Philippides suggests!

In 490 B.C., Darius, the great king of Persia, who had conquered much of the Middle East, invaded Greece. The Persians subdued Attica and marched southward to crush Athens. Herodotus relates:

Before they had yet left the city, the captains sent to Sparta a messenger, Philippides, an Athenian, who was a runner and had practiced this trade. Philippides himself reported to the Athenians that Pan met him on Mount Parthenium above Tages.

Pan called Philippides by name, and commanded him to ask the Athenians why they paid him no attention, though he was well disposed to them and often helped them, and should do so again. Athenians believed it to be trite, but when their affairs had prospered, they founded a temple to Pan beneath the citadel, and ever since his message [to Philippides] they have propitiated him with sacrifices and with a torch race every year.

Philippides ran the 75 miles to Sparta in one day. The Spartans refused aid to Athens. The next day, he ran back – a feat that would task our own marathon runners.

The Athenians attacked the Persians on the plain of Marathon, winning one of the most decisive battles in world history. In *Theseus*, Plutarch records that the Greeks claimed superhuman warriors, Theseus Athene and Heracles, descended to fight with them. Victory was won by aid from the gods.

Herodotus was born only six years after the battle of Marathon, and probably met people who confirmed the tale of Philippides. He would see with his own eyes the temple to Pan, and learn why it was built. Silenus, brother of Pan, a jovial, tipsy old man, was a satyr, possibly a humanoid.

In *Sulla*, Plutarch reports that in 83 B.C., at Apollonia, near Dyrrachium in Illyria, Sulla's soldiers caught a satyr asleep. Despite many interpreters, this humanoid could not understand. He emitted a hoarse cry like a goat. To us, this sylvan creature appears an alien from another world, like those green children manifesting from St. Martin's Land in the Middle Ages, and the strange humanoids said to be manifesting today.

Surely Philippides must have told a most convincing tale to persuade the Athenians to build a temple to Pan! Could he have met a spaceman? Plutarch relates that in the time of Tiberius, 14 A.D., one Thramm, pilot of a ship making for Italy, was thrice called by name and bidden to give the news that Great Pan was dead. A tale with UFO overtones?

The Persians planned revenge for their defeat at Marathon. Ten years later, in 480 B.C., Xerxes invaded Greece with tremendous land and naval forces. Themistocles cleverly lured the great Persian fleet, partly crippled by heavy storms, to venture into the narrow waters about the island of Salamis, watched by Xerxes seated on a marble throne on the hill above.

The heavier Greek ships smashed the trapped enemy in a glorious victory. The following year, the Spartans routed the invaders at Plataea. The Persians were shattered, and Greece saved. Plutarch, in *Themistocles XV*, wrote:

> At this stage of the struggle, they say that a great light flamed out from Eleusis, and the echoing cry filled the Thriassian plain down to the sea... Then out of the shouting throng a cloud seemed to lift itself slowly from the earth, pass out seaward, and settle down upon the triremes.
>
> Others fancied they saw apparitions and shapes of armed men coming from Regina with hands stretched to protect the Hellenic triremes. These they conjectured were the Aeacidae, who had been prayerfully invoked before the battle to come to their aid.

In 1287 B.C., Ramses II, facing defeat by the Hittites at Kadesh, swore the god Amon came to his aid. The Japanese claim that in 660 B.C., the heavenly deities assisted their Emperor Jimmu against the Koreans. Cicero recorded that in 498 B.C., Castor and Pollux saved the Romans at Lake Regillus. A comet, possibly a UFO, hovered over the battle of Hastings in A.D. 1066. Strange aerial lights attended World War II and Korean War battles.

Did gods visit Marathon and Salamis? The great dramatist, Aeschylus, probably thought so. He fought there. During the 5th century B.C., the golden age of Greek drama, the brilliant playwrights of Greece (Aeschylus, Sophocles, Euripides, Aristophanes, etc.) introduced the gods as immortals mingling with men. The intervention of a god to foretell the future or to give judgment was evidently accepted as vaguely possible, if somewhat improbable.

Race memory had implanted in the mind of all Greeks the reality of the gods in ancient times. The cynical younger generation probably looked upon them as exiled royalty living in luxury somewhere in the skies, perhaps even returning occasionally, incognito, to see their friends. The Greek dramatists knew the gods were not mere symbols, but supermen larger than life, with grandiose moods dominating mortal men. Surely the gods were spacemen?

Behind these colossi bestriding Greece, we glimpse in the shadows a few solitary eccentrics who seem more suited to our space age. Those spacemen watching Babylon and Israel must also have landed amidst the mountains of the Peloponnese and met some disciples. Our knowledge is so tantalizingly vague, yet we may imagine the men they would likely contact.

Lycurgus, prince of Sparta, visited Spain, Crete, Libya, Egypt, and even India in the 9th or 10th century before Christ, meeting the wise men of those countries. Lycurgus was hailed as a savior. He paid frequent visits to Delphi, and said the Laws were given him there by Apollo just as Minos, Hammurabbi, and Moses received Laws from their own gods.

The belief that Lycurgus was inspired by Celestials was strengthened by the tradition that after giving the Laws to Sparta, he left to end his life in voluntary exile, just as Lao Tzu – after teaching Taoism to the Chinese – was last seen climbing a mountain toward the clouds.

No one really knows where Lycurgus died. Centuries later, the Spartans believed that Lycurgus was not a man, but a god, and built a temple to him with yearly sacrifices and the highest honors. Like Quetzalcoatl, lawgiver to ancient Mexico, was Lycurgus translated to the skies?

During the 6th century B.C. lived the poet Aethalides, a herald, the son of Mercury, to whom it was granted to be among the dead and the living at stated times. He was said to have traveled in Hades and above Earth, reminiscent of Enoch. This ancient Adamski penned his revelations in a poem unfortunately lost. Pythagoras claimed to be a reincarnation of Aethalides, suggesting the poet was an initiate receptive to spacemen.

Pythagoras, the sage of Samos, who flourished in the 6th century B.C., was acclaimed by Diodorus Siculus as a god among men. He was the first to introduce geometry to Greece from Egypt. The sage preached a simple life, and called his principles Philosophia or Love of Wisdom. He said that because of human weakness, no man is wise, but all men could become "lovers of wisdom" or "philosophers."

Ammianus Marcellinus reported that Pythagoras learned his knowledge from a Hyperborean Druid, Abatis, the priest of Apollo, who took no earthly food and rode through the air on the "arrow of Apollo," suggestive of a spaceman. Pythagoras also told of intercourse with the Gods. People believed the sage to have been miraculously transported around Earth, hinting at his friendship with space beings.

The mysterious disappearances of people in the present-day, and in the past, arouse speculation as to abduction by extraterrestrials. Legends in many countries tell of heroes transported to a land of eternal youth, where they mingle with immortals in wondrous realms beyond space and time, possibly another planet. Sometimes, they return to find their families and friends long dead and buried.

Epimenides, the celebrated poet and prophet of Crete, when a boy in the early 7th century B.C., was sent out by his father in search of a sheep. Seeking shelter from the heat of the midday sun, he went into a cave and there fell into a deep sleep, which lasted 57 years. On his return, he found to his amazement that his brother had grown an old man.

In 596 B.C., invited by Solon to Athens, he worked many wonders in the city. His influence was so profound that 600 years later, St. Paul, in his Epistle to Titus, quoted Epimenides with surprising derision. The Cretans believed that he lived for 300 years and worshipped him as a god. Was his alleged long sleep in a cave an explanation concealing "translation" to another planet, where he was taught cosmic wisdom before returning to Earth?

Another astral traveler was Aristeas of Proconnesis, a noted writer quoted by Longinus, who lived in the 3rd century before Christ. He once vanished from Cyzicus, the wealthy city near the Sea of Marmora, and reappeared at Metapontum, near Taranto, to spread the worship of Apollo. He was an authority on the inaccessible Hyperboreans. It is tempting to wonder whether his travels were made in spaceships.

The scanty evidence would suggest that Lycurgus, Aethalides, Pythagoras, Epimenides, and Aristeas, like their contemporaries, the prophets of Israel, were inspired by spacemen.

The philosophers spoke of the gods somewhat vaguely. Perhaps they hesitated to reveal the esoteric teachings of the mysteries. Generally, they were much more interested in men. Plato, Aristotle, and their followers studied the relation of man to the universe – abstract problems of human conduct, love, justice, education, and practical conceptions of the ideal state.

This was the age of Sophists like Socrates, concerned with ethics and the nature of reality, disputing with the irritated Athenians – not speculating about spacemen. When Socrates spoke of his "daemon," he usually meant the voice of conscience, his inner self.

Plato, however, wrote in *Laws* 713 D: "Daemons are defined as a race superior to men but inferior to gods. They were created to watch human affairs," suggesting perhaps the existence of a celestial race of spacemen. In the *Phaedrus* 146 F, Plato, describing the divine as beauty, goodness, and the like, added: "Zeus, the mighty leader, holding the reins of a winged chariot, leads the way in heaven, ordering ill and taking care of ill."

This concept would suggest that Plato believed in celestials speeding across the skies, like the gods in their golden cars so brilliantly described in the Sanskrit classics.

Lysander, the distinguished Spartan general, in 405 B.C. brought the Peloponnesian War to a conclusion by defeating the Athenian fleet at Aegospotami near the Dardanelles. Plutarch, in his *Life of Lysander*, describing the battle, wrote:

> Therefore some actually thought the result due to divine intervention. There were some who declared that the Dioscuri (Castor and Pollux) appeared as twin stars on either side of Lysander's ship, just as he was sailing out against the enemy and shone out over the ruddersweeps.

Diodorus Siculus, commenting on the fall of Sparta in 372 B.C., wrote:

> A divine portent foretold the loss of their empire, for there was seen in the heavens, during the course of many nights, a great blazing torch, which was named from its shape a "flaming beam," and a little later, to the surprise of all, the Spartans were defeated in a great battle and irretrievably lost their supremacy.

Callisthenes recorded that a similar appearance of a trail of fire was observed before the sea swallowed up Buris and Helice, cities in Achaia, in 373 B.C. Diodorus Siculus also referred to a celestial torch appearing when earthquakes and floods destroyed cities in the Peloponnese. Aristotle, then only 11 years old, swore it was a comet.

Alexander the Great, whose death in 323 B.C., at thirty-three, left the world and himself unconquered, in masterly campaigns led the Greeks to India, as Napoleon's ill-starred venture to the Nile resurrected the buried glories of Egypt. Scholars accompanying the expedition fertilized the genius of Hellas with the age-old wisdom of the East.

A marveling posterity adulated the hero with prodigies. He actually thought himself to be a god. His dazzling meteoric career certainly suggests powerful inspiration from some inner "daemon" or other celestial source.

Arrian, Ptolemy, and Megasthenes depict Alexander's life and death in prosaic detail. Later historians embellished him with wonders of doubtful authenticity omitted in the classical histories. Frank Edwards, the noted American UFO investigator, quoting some anonymous source, states:

> He tells of two strange craft that dived repeatedly until the war elephants, the men and the horses, all panicked and refused to cross the river. What did the things look like? His historian describes them as great shining, silvery shields spitting fire around the rims – things that came from the skies and returned to the skies.

This remarkable incident was paralleled by an equally fantastic visitation during the siege of Tyre by Alexander in 332 B.C. Alberto Fenoglio, the erudite Italian scholar, possibly quoting Giovanni Gustavo Droysen's *Storia Di Alessandro il Grande*, revealed a startling incident. I translate his amazing account as follows:

> The fortress would not yield. Its walls were fifty feet high, and constructed so solidly that no siege-engine was able to damage it. The Tyrians disposed of the greatest technicians and builders of war-machines of the time, and they intercepted in the air the incendiary arrows and projectiles hurled by the catapults on the city.
>
> One day, suddenly there appeared over the Macedonian camp these "flying shields," as they had been called, which flew in triangular formation, led by an exceedingly large one, the others were smaller by almost a half. In all there were five. The unknown chronicler narrates that they circled slowly over Tyre, while thousands of warriors on both sides stood and watched them in astonishment.
>
> Suddenly from the largest "shield" came a lightning flash that struck the walls. These crumbled, other flashes followed, and walls and towers dissolved, as if they had been built of mud, leaving the way open for the besiegers, who poured like an avalanche through the breaches. The "flying shields" hovered over the city until it was completely stormed, then they very swiftly disappeared aloft, soon melting into the blue sky.

The intervention of "flying shields" from heaven during a siege was chronicled again about 1100 years later. In his curious mediaeval Latin, Monk Lawrence, in *Annales Laurissenses*, wrote how a few years earlier, in A.D. 776, the heathen Saxons rebelled against Charlemagne and having destroyed the castle at Aeresburg, marched down the river Lenne to besiege Sigiburg. As the Saxons pounded the castle with great stones from their catapults and prepared final assault against the outnumbered Christians:

> The glory of god appeared in manifestation above the church within the fortress. Those watching outside the place, of whom many still live to this very day, said they beheld the likeness of two large shields, reddish in color, in motion, flaming above the church, and when the pagans who were outside saw this sign, they were at once thrown into confusion, and terrified with great fear, they began to flee from the castle.

In panic, the multitudes of Saxons were driven to headlong flight. Later, they submitted to Charlemagne. The heathens were so impressed by the power of the "Lord," conjured down by the Christians, that they begged to be baptized. Monk Lawrence, marveling at this divine prodigy, expressly mentions that many eyewitnesses were still alive to confirm its reality.

Such astounding incidents in the times of Alexander the Great and Charlemagne confound our conditioned thought-patterns, though we solemnly worship those extraterrestrials manifesting in Israel. Are these celestial interventions not credible?

Suppose if, in the next century, our cosmonauts visiting Mars chance on some battle being waged beneath! May they not perhaps swoop down, flashing laser rays, to aid one side or the other? The victors will worship their saviors as Gods; the vanquished shall curse them as devils. Is that what happened once here on Earth? An intriguing problem for our theologians…

Whatever discourses astronomers and philosophers might hold on the existence of the Gods, the people of Greece, with superstitious awe, firmly believed the stars were inhabited by wonderful eccentrics who might be cajoled to aid mortals on Earth.

SPACEMEN IN THE ANCIENT WEST: THE FAIR GOD

Mexico City stands on the site of Tenochtitlán, the Aztec capital ravaged by Cortes and his gold-hungry conquistadores. The Aztecs believed that long ago, their ancestors, the first men, emerged from Seven Caverns at Chicomoztoc, a tradition shared by the Native Americans, the Quiches and the Incas, suggesting refuge underground from cataclysm or aerial war.

Traditions recall that the Aztecs, the People of the Crane, about 1160 A.D., were directed by their Sun God, Huitzilopochtli, to leave their home at Aztlan, far north of the Colorado River, and migrate southward to the promised land indicated by an island in a lake, where they would see an "eagle devouring a serpent."

Six of the tribes bearing an image of their god came to the Land of Anahuac and for decades, followed the Spirit of Huitzilopochtli, manifesting as a white eagle, which led them in confusion, like Jehovah leading the children of Israel for forty years in the wilderness – a significant parallel, especially if both the Aztec and Hebrew gods were spacemen. The "white eagle" leading the Aztecs may have been a spaceship.

Finally, about 1325 A.D., the descendants of the original wanderers arrived on the shore of Lake Tezcoco, where they saw an eagle perched on a cactus, its talons clutching a snake; the tribes halted and the priests scanned the heavens, awaiting God's command.

Huitzilopochtli ordered the Aztecs to build here their city, Tenochtitlán, called "Mexico" by the Europeans after the war god, Mexitili, from which the Aztecs would "expand to a prosperous empire and conquer the earth."

These symbols of the sun god, eagle and serpent, evoke the legend of the postdiluvian Babylonian king, Etana, associated with an eagle and serpent, who flew to the skies. The eagle and serpent symbolize the wisdom of the sky god, and feature prominently in worldwide religions (i.e., the Garuda of Asia, the Thunderbird of the Pacific Northwest, the Roc of the Middle East, etc.).

The long trek of the Aztecs during the 13th century, led by priests inspired by signs from heaven, is strangely similar to those familiar stories of the patriarchs in the Old Testament following the "power and glory of the Lord." Even today, Mexico's national emblem is an eagle on a cactus grasping a serpent.

Who was Quetzalcoatl, whose beneficence inspired the people of Mexico for hundreds and probably thousands of years, and whose emblem, the feathered serpent, dominated monuments and temples of Central America? The Italian Jesuit, Francisco Javier Clavijero Echegaray, described Quetzalcoatl as high priest of Tula, center of Toltec culture:

> He was white in complexion, tall and corpulent, broad in forehead, with large eyes, long black hair, thick beard; a man of austere and exemplary life, clothed in long garments, gentle and prudent. He was expert in the art of melting metals and polishing precious stones, which he taught the Tultecans.

Fray Juan de Torquemada, the 16th century Franciscan missionary, described him as fair and ruddy with long hair. Like his 20 companions, he was dressed in a long robe of black linen, cut low at the neck with short sleeves – a dress worn by natives to this very day. The reign of Quetzalcoatl was the golden age of Mexico.

The origin of the Fair God mystified the Aztecs and outraged the Spaniards, who were startled at his close affinity with Christ. Today, myth merges with history. His identity intrigues us more acutely than ever, as Quetzalcoatl surely symbolizes the landing of spacemen. Identification of this great cultural hero varies from cosmic grandeur to folk romance. The truth must be sought from his name, which evokes that mellifluent language of Atlantis.

The *quetzal* was a rare bird with green feathers. *Coatl* is a combination of the Nahua word for "snake" or "serpent," *co*, and the Nahua word *atl*, meaning "water" – together signifying "winged serpent." The Mayas called him "Kukulkan," the Quiches of Guatemala as "Gucumatz." He was known to the Aztecs as "Ehecatl" or "God of the Air," and "Nanihehecatl" or "Lord of the Four Wings." His most intriguing title "Tlahuizcalpantecuhtli," the "Lord of Light of Dawn," identifies him with Venus.

Legends state that Quetzalcoatl's mother was the virgin Coatlicue. His father was the sun, resembling the divine birth of all saviors. One version alleges that his mother swallowed an emerald, the green jewel occultically associated with the planet Venus. Traditions vaguely agree that Quetzalcoatl was a wise king who suddenly appeared from the east, bringing the arts of civilization, law, healing, the calendar and writing, and also maize to the Nahuas, early inhabitants of the Mexican plateau.

Like Buddha, he taught men compassion and cosmic wisdom, the message of love and peace with a sublime reverence, far transcending the bloodthirsty rites degenerate priests were later to perpetrate in his name.

The Toltec myths state that Quetzalcoatl ruled men in wondrous peace and prosperity, like the golden age of Saturn, and those idyllic times mentioned in the Egyptian, Indian, and Chinese classics. Envious of such good fortune, Tezcatlipoca, god of the air, worshipped by the invading Nahuas, plotted his downfall. Their rivalry vaguely recalls the conflict between Osiris and Set, Saturn and Zeus.

With a cunning suggestive of the Scandinavian Loki causing the death of Baldur, Tezcatlipoca, disguised as a white-haired old man, induced Quetzalcoatl, temporarily paralyzed, to drink a healing potion so efficacious that the hero recovered with sufficient virility to seduce his own sister, Quetzalpetlatl.

In remorse at this fall from grace, Quetzalcoatl decided he must return to the sun. After a sad farewell to his sorrowful people, he sailed westward on a raft of serpents to the fabled land of Tlapallan, the country of bright colors. It intrigues us to wonder whether the raft of serpents was a spaceship whose forcefield flashing electric discharges could perhaps be symbolized by serpents.

This speculation is enhanced by another legend, which tells how the god flung himself on a funeral pyre, and from the flames ascended to the planet Venus, evoking those translations describing the skies of Hercules, Enoch, Elijah, and Romulus. The Mexican *Codex Borgia* states that the evening star, Venus, was associated by the Nahuas with Quetzalcoatl and the solar disc. Quetzalcoatl was occasionally regarded as the sun god, but more often pictured as if emerging from the sun, his dwelling place.

Conventional interpretation may be wrong. Perhaps the paintings depict a god alighting from a flying saucer? Fantastic though it seems, this suggestion is surely more logical than the idea that Quetzalcoatl came from the sun itself, admittedly a belief that some early Christians associated with Christ.

Temples to Quetzalcoatl were circular in shape, generally thought to signify the *yoni*, the feminine sexual orifice honored in the old fertility cults. However, there is a growing suspicion that the ancient stone circles inspiring religious architecture actually represented spaceships. South America, particularly the Marcahuasi Plateau, abounds with evidence of spacemen in ancient times. Like Osiris, Jehovah, Saturn, and Indra, Quetzalcoatl could have manifested in Mexico by spaceship.

Mythologists doubt the reality of Osiris, Indra, Zeus and Woden. They dismiss these gods as anthropomorphisms of natural forces, humanized by the primitive peoples of antiquity. Historians generally agree that one or more cultural heroes called Quetzalcoatl really did suddenly appear, teaching a brilliant civilization to Central and South America.

Many rulers in Mexico and Peru, like kings in Europe and Asia, deliberately destroyed ancient records so that their people could not learn of the past. Such vandalism obliged the priests to preserve their lore in hieroglyphics, whose esoteric concepts were incomprehensible to the uninitiated. The few writings that did exist were burned by the Spaniards as works of the Devil, until Jesuit Fathers, Sahagun, Diaz, Torquemada, and other scholars sought to preserve the native traditions.

The mystery of Quetzalcoatl has challenged many distinguished authorities, and caused widely divergent theories. Shortly after the conquest, Alva de Ixtlilxochitl, an Aztec chronicler, compiled notable annals wherein he declared that Quetzalcoatl succeeded the defeated giants and lived during the third age, El Sol de Viente (the Sun of the Wind), contemporary with Lemuria – a view advanced by Dr. George Hunt Williamson and James Churchward (who suggested 32,000 B.C.).

Harold T. Wilkins and Marcel F. Homet believed he was an Atlantean "divine man" from about 11,000 B.C. Hyatt and Verrill identify Quetzalcoatl as Naram-Sin, who led an expedition from Babylon to South America before 2,000 B.C. Constance Itwin considers the Fair God to have been a Phoenician around 600 B.C.

L. Taylor Hansen's 24 years of research quotes several fascinating legends, and concludes the "Katezahl" was an Essene, perhaps a witness to the crucifixion of Jesus, who sailed to America in a Roman ship, approximating the Catholic belief that he was St. Thomas.

Mexican archaeologists reject all these claims, and estimate that Quetzalcoatl led the Mayas to Yucatan in A.D. 967. The Mayas know the great white stranger as "Kukulkan," the Peruvians as "Viracocha," the Columbians as "Bochicha," the Quiches as "Gucumatz," and the Polynesians as "Wakee." He was known under many names by the Indians of North America.

Scholars quote impressive evidence to support their rival claims for Quetzalcoatl; such contradictions surely prove that in folk memory, this cultural hero represents the many white strangers who, down through the ages, appeared in Mexico and Peru to teach the arts and crafts of civilization – as they taught the peoples of most countries all over the earth.

All the chroniclers agree that the initial success of the Spanish invasion in 1519, which could have been smashed, was ensured by Montezuma's superstitious conviction that Cortes was Quetzalcoatl, returned to chasten Mexico with that tribulation he had threatened long ago.

CHAPTER 15

One researcher's bold hypothesis that space intelligences used the power of the stars to begin the human race!

ANCIENT "SPACE GODS" AND THE BIRTH OF MAN – JACQUES BERGIER – 1976

Seventy million years ago, the earth was inhabited by giant reptiles, gigantic lizards, colossal saurians, huge creatures that slithered, swam, flew. Their reign lasted 100 million years; whereas, according to the most optimistic estimates, man has had barely six million years.

This means that these species of reptiles had more time to adapt and evolve than man. Furthermore, it is impossible to pretend that they represented an evolutionary failure. Any species that lasts 100 million years must be considered "successfully" adapted. Yet few species that were contemporaries of those reptiles survive – for example, certain crabs, which have not changed in 300 million years.

In fact, in less than one million years, the giant reptiles entirely disappeared. How, and why?

We can scarcely maintain that it was because of a change in climate, for even when the climate changes, the oceans hardly vary, and many of these reptiles lived in the oceans.

It is impossible to believe that a higher form of life was able to exterminate them. This would have required a considerable army, whose traces we would certainly have found.

One amusing hypothesis is that our ancestors, the mammals, might have fed on dinosaur eggs. But it is only that: an amusing hypothesis; the ichthyosaurs deposited their eggs in the oceans, out of their adversaries' reach.

It has been said that the grasses changed, and that the new grasses were too tough for the big reptiles – a completely unlikely hypothesis. Large numbers of vegetation types survived, on which they could have fed perfectly well. The giant tortoises of the Galapagos Islands, the ones that interested Darwin so much, did not die of hunger.

One could say that species grow old, become senile, and die, but this is bad logic. The preservation of the genetic code prevents a species from dying out. And why haven't those species that are still living after several hundred millions of years, such as crabs and cockroaches, become senile, too?

None of these hypotheses hold. But something happened. What then?

An ingenious hypothesis has been outlined by two Soviet scientists, V.I. Krasovkii and I.S. Shlovsky, both of whom are eminent astrophysicists – especially the latter, who is the author of some extremely important works in astrophysics and radio astronomy. It was Shlovsky, in fact, who studied synchrotron radiation, and showed that relatively rapid and extremely violent events can be produced at the center of galaxies, as well as in space in general.

The two Soviet scientists explain the end of the dinosaurs by hypothesizing a star explosion that occurred at a relatively small distance from our solar system – a supernova at five or 10 parsecs from us, which would have increased the density of radiations coming from space.

Lending credibility to this theory, the English radio astronomer, Hanbury Brown, believes he has detected traces of the explosion of a supernova 50,000 years ago, at a distance of only 40 parsecs from our solar system.

Two U.S. scientists, K.D. Terry of the University of Kansas and W.H. Tucker of Rice University, have recently given close quantitative study to the problem. They have observed stars that actually produced such radiation bombardments when they exploded. The effect of a bombardment varies according to the intensity of the earth's magnetic field at the time.

This field partially protects us from the bombardment of cosmic particles, by turning away those with a magnetic charge and forcing them into orbit around our planet. But this magnetic field varies in intensity. Right now, it is on a downswing, and will reach a low point at about the 36th century A.D.

It is possible that 70 million years ago, a violent bombardment may have coincided with a diminution in the earth's magnetic field, bringing about a wave of mutations, in which the dinosaurs died and man's ancestors were born.

According to an East German scientist, Richter, the bombardment originated at the center of our galaxy and was extremely powerful, in spite of being produced at such a considerable distance.

If we accept this theory, as we well may, we still must ask: what caused the massive explosion? I first outlined my explanation in 1957 during a broadcast on French television. I still remember the uproar that followed, and I still stand by my hypothesis: that the star explosion that killed the dinosaurs was deliberately induced, designed to set off a slow process of evolution leading to intelligent life – in essence, that we were created by extremely powerful beings.

Knowledgeable both of the laws of physics and of the laws of genetics, these beings – who could truly be called gods – set in motion a series of events that will not stop with man, but will continue until this evolution results in other gods – beings equal to their creators.

Obviously, this hypothesis is very bold. More than once already, however, we have speculated on the existence of beings infinitely more powerful than ourselves. We have even offered quantitative estimates on what their technologies might be.

The greatest source of energy, which is demonstrated in the H-bomb, is the conversion of hydrogen to helium. Now the amount of hydrogen in the oceans is enormous, but there is even more in the sun. We can certainly imagine beings capable of extracting hydrogen from the sun and using it. Theoreticians call these "Type III" civilizations.

What has become of these civilizations? Do they still exist in the universe?

Many fine minds are answering this question affirmatively. Shlovsky considers it a not entirely farfetched hypothesis that quasars and pulsars – currently unexplained celestial objects – may be signs of *biological* activity. The Soviet scientist believes we should examine the sky systematically for what he calls "miracles" – that is, phenomena that cannot be explained solely by known natural laws or by imaginative extrapolations of those laws.

Among these phenomena, Shlovsky would place: the abnormal behavior of Phobos, the satellite of Mars that, according to him, might be an artificial construction; and the observation of a particular type of star, type R, which produces a short-lived element that does not exist in nature: technetium. This condition has suggested to eminent scientists the possibility that intelligent beings are bombarding these type R stars with technetium to produce a signal.

Other serious investigators – Carl Sagan, for example – believe that beings of Type III civilizations can modulate the electromagnetic emissions of a star as easily as we modulate those of a transmitter of sound and pictures. In fact, a group of Soviet researchers, under the direction of astrophysicists Kardaschev and Pschenko, are currently investigating such signals.

This group believes that, considering the various static disturbances that affect Earth's atmosphere, it will be necessary to place a radio observatory on the dark side of the moon in order to detect these signals. In any case, their calculations have demonstrated to them that with completely conceivable means of energy, signals can be sent up a distance of 13,000 parsecs – in other words, to a greater distance than that which separates us from the center of the galaxy.

A U.S. astrophysicist, Freeman J. Dyson, envisages an even more fantastic "miracle" in the sky. He believes that there exist beings that can utilize the entirety of energy produced by their star. These beings must no longer be living on planets; instead, they inhabit artificial spheres that they have built themselves, and which totally surround their star.

Other "miracles," it seems, have been observed in the sky. Though they are rarely mentioned in scientific publications because they seem too fantastic, you hear them talked about at astronomical congresses, during meals and in the corridors. For example, there is speculation concerning certain multiple star systems that might be composed of stars of different ages – that is to say, stars coupled necessarily as a result of intelligent activity.

We see, therefore, that the existence in the universe of beings much more powerful than ourselves is being taken as a serious possibility. It is being quantitatively envisaged by eminent scientists.

We need not add to these speculations. We should simply note that the human form perhaps ought not to be rejected. It is possible that it is one of the major stable forms of intelligence in the universe. We do not even utilize one-tenth of our brains.

Our civilization is far from being perfect. We do not have the least idea of what a civilization would be like in which human beings used 100 percent of their brain capacity. And it is not at all absurd to attribute to such a civilization in the stars, if it exists, powers analogous to those of Type III civilizations.

Such a point of view seems more plausible to me than all the inventions of science fiction. But be that as it may, my intention is not to study the possible forms of extraterrestrial beings, but rather what I believe to be their manifestations.

To me, the first of these manifestations might have had, as its result, the end of the dinosaurs. Considering that Earth's evolution had been heading down a dead end – that there had not been any progress with the giant reptiles for 50 million years – the space intelligences, wanting perhaps to increase the number of their "brothers in reason" (an expression of the great Soviet mathematician Kolmogoroff), reversed the direction of this evolution, and set up a new evolutionary goal.

We do not, for the moment, know to what it is leading; but it would be absurd to believe that man, as he is today, was the end they were pursuing.

Perhaps the intelligences will be forced to wipe out our species and set another chain in motion. This may be an inspired intuition. In any case, the intelligences seem far removed from H.P. Lovecraft's Great Old Men, who created life on the earth by mistake, or as a joke.

With this concept in mind, it is interesting to note that intelligent signals have been spotted coming from celestial object CTA 102. At least the wavelength of these signals has been calculated as coming from the vicinity of CTA 102, and it has been established that they contain the fundamental wavelength of the universe, the radiation transmitted by interstellar hydrogen.

Since that discovery, Prof. Gerald Feinberg of the New York Academy of Sciences has advanced the opinion that these signals are transmitted by particles that he calls *tachyons*, from a Greek word meaning "rapid" – particles that can be conveyed in the void of space more rapidly than light, without any contradiction of Einstein's theory.

When methods for observing and detecting the tachyons are perfected, we will probably receive signals being transmitted by other races whose evolution also was set in motion by the star that killed the dinosaurs. And perhaps we will detect the observation devices of the intelligences, who are most certainly observing us in the same way we observe microbe cultures under a microscope.

Although we have some precise notions of the energy sources the intelligences might have had available for making their experiments – sources that are extensions of those we ourselves are using in our experiments on the hydrogen and antimatter bombs – our knowledge in the area of genetics is still too vague for us to be able to imagine how directed mutations could be produced at a distance.

We first need to know how mutations can be directed. In order to produce directed mutations, a radiation of very short wavelength, or particles with very high energy, would have to be employed.

It would next be necessary to modulate this transmission, in order to transfer genetic characteristics on this modulation, in the same way that images are transferred by a television channel. Calculations will show that this is possible, provided that very short particles on the Broglie wavelength, or on the short gamma ray band, are used.

Indeed, it is possible for us to conceive of a laboratory apparatus (for example, a laser) regulated to produce the kind of radiations that would induce mutations. But when we try to imagine a mutation on the scale of a star, created and modulated by the intelligences, our imaginations fail. A virus would undoubtedly have the same difficulty trying to imagine a laser.

The creatures that built and modulated the star that killed the dinosaurs really were gods. They are probably the same intelligences that regulate, to a hundred billionth, the frequency of those celestial objects called pulsars. The fact is that more and more scientists admit, in private, that the pulsars are artificial – so many, indeed, that this hypothesis will probably soon appear publicly in most official publications.

Having noted this, we must recognize that most signs of the intelligences' activity must escape us for the moment. In the same way that whole civilizations have lived without knowing about the radio, or of the existence of other solar systems, we will very probably remain unaware of highly important phenomena that, were we able to detect them, would undoubtedly prove to us the existence of other civilizations.

It is equally possible that perfectly classic phenomena may in reality be, without our suspecting it, manifestations of intelligent activity. In this regard, I can cite two hypotheses.

John W. Campbell, the late physicist and science-fiction writer, studied cosmic particles – particles reaching us from space, endowed with very high levels of energy, capable of reaching 10 electron-volts. These particles are made of element groups with which we are familiar, ranging from hydrogen to iron.

But this very ordinary matter is launched abruptly, at a formidable speed, as if a fraction of interstellar gas had suddenly been accelerated until it reached speeds bordering the speed of light. The mechanism that produced this acceleration remains unknown, although Fermi, Shlovsky, and many other scientists have offered different models.

Campbell, for his part, suggested that the universe is full of spaceships that are moving at speeds close to that of light. As these ships sweep interstellar gas before them, we observe a trail – a wake – that is none other than the cosmic rays we have detected.

It cannot be said that Campbell's hypothesis has exactly been received with delirious enthusiasm by physicists. However, one American physicist, Robert Bussard, has suggested a model for an interstellar ship that would absorb interstellar gas by means of a scoop placed in the bow, from which it would obtain energy through fusion, and would then utilize the products of the reactions – such as propulsion fluid – with the propellant then being ejected through the stern.

If the universe is full of this sort of spaceship linking the stars, then Campbell was right. (And that happened to him exasperatingly often.) We can also imagine perfectly well that the mysterious variable objects called pulsars are beacons guiding these interstellar ships in the night of space.

A second hypothesis comes from Russian scientific writer, Ekaterina Zouravieva. According to Ms. Zouravieva, we constantly receive signals from space, signals that were sent at the birth of humanity and undoubtedly well before that. This signal is made up of the aurora borealis and the aurora australis (the northern and southern lights).

Whatever the truth or otherwise of these two examples, the principle of the hypotheses is probably good, even if their authors do not take themselves too seriously. Shlovsky had cause to observe one day, in a conversation with friends, that there are two kinds of hypotheses: the working hypothesis, intended to serve as a point of departure for study; and the conversational hypothesis, which serves to pass the time agreeably between two meetings on the mathematics of interstellar plasma.

The basic hypothesis of this article – that we are the result of a series of mutations set off from the outside – is a working hypothesis; the presence of messages to be decoded in an aurora borealis is a conversational hypothesis.

What other solar systems, or at least what other stars possessing solar systems, could have been influenced by the artificial source of energy that killed the dinosaurs?

If we go a reasonable distance from our solar system – for instance, 15 light years – we find five systems: Alpha Centauri, Epsilon Eridani, 61 Cygni A, Epsilon Indi, and Tau Ceti. In centuries to come, research will undoubtedly be carried out to see if life exists in these systems. If it does, it will be interesting to find out if this life resembles ours, and if the rocks on the planets of these systems bear traces of a cosmic bombardment that was produced, on our scale, 70 million years ago.

With such a second fix, we could then locate in space the star, either artificial or artificially controlled, that killed the dinosaurs.

Until we have such a cross-reference, unfortunately, we are unlikely to discover our "founding" star. Within a distance of 1,000 light years, we find approximately 10 million stars, and it is currently impossible to know which of these might be the dead debris of an artificial star created by the intelligences.

The destruction of the dinosaurs certainly came from the cosmos and not from our solar system, but the study of cosmic influences connected to the galaxy is still in its infancy. We have been able to observe numerical coincidences, which are perhaps only coincidences. (For instance, the frequency of the great glacial periods, about 250 million years, corresponds roughly to the rotation period of our solar system around the center of the galaxy, which is about 230 million years.)

An attempt is also being made to determine the frequency at which the center of our galaxy, where chain star explosions and disturbances are produced of which we have only a very faint idea, throws off sprays of condensed matter. Unfortunately, we still have far to go in this study, though interesting discoveries are being made.

For example, it is being debated whether or not it is the chain star explosions that are at the origin of the mysterious quasars, which are scarcely more bulky than single stars, and which liberate as much energy as whole galaxies. It is generally admitted that these quasars are something completely new, and that it is currently impossible to envisage a scientific hypothesis that could render an account of them.

Some scientists think that humanity might one day be able to understand and even reproduce the energy source of these quasars. This is one of the justifications for the fantastic budgets swallowed up by such organizations as CERN (European Center for Nuclear Research). For myself, I feel that humanity is already menaced with destruction by nuclear weapons, and that a brake must be put on research institutes, which might put at our disposal fantastic powers that the human race is not yet ready for.

The ancient alchemists were completely right in believing that the secrets of matter had to be jealously guarded. If Hitler had had the means of exploding a star the way the intelligences exploded the star that killed the dinosaurs, he would certainly have done so. Therefore, I hope that studies of very high energies will not succeed for some time, and that the power to kindle and extinguish stars freely will never be entrusted to the military or to politicians.

We have already made, in going from TNT to the hydrogen bomb, a colossal jump. A hydrogen bomb weighing one ton can liberate an amount of energy equal to that of 10 million tons of TNT. This is what we call a 10-megaton bomb, and, of course, bombs of this sort actually exist. A comparable jump would be needed to take us from the energy of the H-bomb to the energy necessary for inducing the explosion of a star.

Thus I hope that this development will not happen during my lifetime. Humanity has proved, all too well, what it is capable of. But to believe that this progress will never occur, in a universe that has existed at least 20 billion years, is extremely naïve.

Somewhere in the universe, viruses evolved into intelligences. If the phenomenon occurred several times, the different intelligences must have come into contact; as Teilhard de Chardin said, "Everything that rises must converge."

A botanist at Harvard, Elso Barghoorn, has proved that certain bacteria lived on Earth three billion years ago. It has required this time, and the assistance of the intelligences, to lead from these bacteria to us, and even if it takes 10 billion years for the Intelligences to appear naturally, this time would only be half the observable age of the universe.

There is nothing in known science that conflicts with theories concerning the existence of the intelligences. There is no longer anything conflicting with the possibility that they may have intervened.

Perhaps they have set up a detection and observation satellite in our solar system – perhaps Phobos, the mysterious satellite of the planet Mars. Perhaps they have set up those protective radiation belts around the earth, which we are just beginning to discover.

Perhaps.